YOU

A BIRTHING PLACE for HEAVEN?

YOUR HOME

A BIRTHING PLACE for HEAVEN?

Warren Henderson

GOSPEL FOLIO PRESS
304 Killaly St. West, Port Colborne, ON L3K 6A6
Available in the UK from JOHN RITCHIE LTD.
40 Beansburn, Kilmarnock, Scotland

YOUR HOME—A BIRTHING PLACE FOR HEAVEN?
by Warren Henderson
Copyright © 2002
All rights reserved

Published by Gospel Folio Press
304 Killaly St. West
Port Colborne, ON L3K 6A6
   ISBN 1-882701-73-9

ORDERING INFORMATION:
Gospel Folio Press
Phone: 1-905-835-9166
E-mail: orders@gospelfolio.com

Printed in Canada

Table of Contents

Introduction

Do you consider your living room furniture or your kitchen table as placed by the side of life's road, an ideal spot to direct souls heavenward? Can you envision your home being a birthing place for heaven and yourself a spiritual midwife? Imagine for a moment the heavenly scene as you share the gospel of Christ with an unsaved soul at your kitchen table. Myriads of angels are peering down from heavenly realms with eager anticipation of celebrating a birth into God's family. What about it? Would you enjoy being used to cause heaven to erupt in jubilation? Do you see your earthly abode as a God-given resource to be used for building His abode, the church? Are you being a good steward of this resource?

Your Home—A Birthing Place for Heaven? has been written to inspire those considering hosting or leading a small group Bible study, and also to encourage and aid those already laboring in this special ministry. Not only do the angels rejoice in heaven when one repentant sinner receives salvation (Lk. 15:10), but there is tremendous joy to the one declaring the gospel truth also (Jn. 3:29). Watching as hungry, needy souls find fulfillment and satisfaction in the Lord Jesus Christ is one of the most exciting experiences in life. Not only is he who wins souls wise (Prov. 11:30), but what a blessing to realize that his life has counted for eternity.

This book provides a short history and evaluation of the present small group movement, which has gained tremendous momentum over the past thirty years. From this evaluation, we will learn what techniques have been profitable in reaching the lost, which have faltered and why. Is there a widespread re-emergence of New Testament Christianity today? What are the dangers, pitfalls, and blessings of the present-day small group movement?

If you have any of the following questions on your mind, this book is for you: How do I know if God is calling me to lead a Bible study? What are the biblical principles for evangelizing my friends, co-workers and neighbors? How do I invite and encourage them to come to a home or workplace study? How do I get started? How does one become a good study leader? How do I lead individuals into a personal relationship with the Lord Jesus Christ and then encourage them to grow and mature in their faith? What study materials do I use? How do I handle difficult situations like personality conflicts or an argumentative person?

Besides these important questions, I will share with the reader a list of "lessons learned" from personal experiences while leading Bible studies. These are practical tips which will help the reader to glean from successes and failures in this type of ministry. May God stimulate you through the reading of this book to use your living room, your kitchen table, or a workplace conference room to introduce weary, thirsty souls to the only satisfying answer in Christ!

1

A Brief History of the Small Group Movement

The small group Bible study actually finds its roots in the practices of the New Testament Church where Christians gathered in one locale in the name of the Lord Jesus (1 Cor. 5:4). These meetings were characterized by simplicity: breaking bread, teaching, praying and fellowship, according to Acts 2:42. Often, it was the home which first provided the opportunity for evangelistic outreach and the discipleship of new converts (Acts 16:14-15; 16:30-34; and likely Acts 18:24-26). These homes often became the birthplaces of new local churches, places where Christians assembled (Rom. 16:5; Philemon 2; Col. 4:15).

History records a consistent remnant of Christians who have gathered in this simple way from the dawn of the Church age through the dark days of deadly human traditions to the present time. Those faithful to New Testament principles of gathering held their ground against the rise of the clergy and an aristocratic form of church government in the late second century AD. They have withstood the traditions of men and pagan practices from the time of Constantine (4th century AD) until the reemergence of an evangelizing Christian minority in the 17th century. In this time period, millions of Christians were slaughtered for holding to biblical Christianity instead of "Churchianity."

By the late 18th and early 19th century, small autonomous groups of Christians were again gathering in significant numbers with the same simplicity which the early church enjoyed. Many groups of Christians were employing small group Bible studies to reach out to the unsaved, to disciple new converts and rediscover lost doctrines. Through the work of itinerant preachers and small group studies (or "cottage meetings" as they were often called), the church experienced much growth during this period. *Christianity Today* magazine provides a concise historical summary of the small group activity at that time, and how it has evolved into the present movement:

> One of the most visible and most researched expressions of North American small groups came to be John Wesley's class meetings. Howard Snyder, in *The Radical Wesley and Patterns for Church Renewal,* outlines Wesley's organizational plan: Wesley started with societies (based on large geographical area), which were subdivided into groups of twelve members called classes. Those within a class who professed assurance of salvation were organized into bands. Finally, band members who 'appeared to be making marked progress toward inward and outward holiness' were formed into intimate cell groups called select societies.
>
> According to Snyder, "The class meeting was the cornerstone of the whole edifice. The classes were in effect house churches—not classes for instruction as the term class might suggest—meeting in the various neighborhoods where the people lived." These classes usually met weekly.
>
> For various historical reasons, class-meeting momentum waned,

but not without forging a critical link in Methodism's growth. The denominational forerunner of today's United Methodist Church was one of the dominant religious bodies in the United States from the mid-1800s to the 1950s.

By the late 1800's, the Sunday School movement was gaining national prominence, in the 1920's becoming the dominant small-group movement in America. Because it was not limited to one or two denominations, it dwarfed the scope of Wesley's class meeting.

"By 1900," says Lyman Coleman, developer of Serendipity Bible-study resources, "the Sunday School movement had developed a cradle-to-the-grave emphasis with a graded curriculum based on the public-school format. By 1950, seventy-five percent of church members were involved in the Sunday School. It was the major force for evangelism and assimilation in the church."

The 1940s and 1950s also gave rise to a number of unrelated parachurch movements: the Oxford group, Alcoholics Anonymous, Faith at Work, the Navigators, InterVarsity and numerous others. Says Coleman, by the 1960s, and even more so by the 1970s, the Sunday School, with its emphasis on age categories, on-site location, and Sunday-only meetings, was clearly in decline. At the same time, a new model was rising, with an emphasis on "life-stage categories," on or off premises meetings, and—to borrow from a recent term of Lyle Schaller—the seven-day-a-week-church.[1]

Yet, the small group environment has undergone even more drastic change over the last forty years. The group-oriented Sunday School classes in the 1960s gave way to the home fellowship groups in the 1970s, which were overcome by support/recovery groups in the 1980s. These mutated into a smorgasbord of diversity in the 1990s. The Wuthnow/Gallup statistics confirm this 1990s diversity. Small groups include 800,000 Sunday School classes (involving 18-22 million people), 900,000 Bible study groups (15-20 million people), 500,000 self-help groups

(8-10 million), 250,000 political/current-events groups (5-10 million), and 250,000 sports/hobby event groups (5-10 million).[2]

Robert Wuthnow reports, "At present, four out of every ten Americans belong to a small group that meets regularly and provides caring and support for it members."[3] These small groups include many facets such as: Bible study, divorce recovery, addiction recovery, singles' groups, book discussion groups, and fishing clubs. Each group strives to gather likeminded people who can regain a sense of community—something that has been generally lost in our society.

On the spiritual scene, one of the most popular small group meetings today is the "cell" church. This is a local church body that meets perhaps weekly as a whole and then more often in small "cell" groups for Bible study and prayer. Sometimes these cell groups take on more appealing names like "Family Life Home Groups." The cell church group has three main ingredients: small size (to ensure Christian intimacy and accountability), simple agenda (to allow the group to be dynamic—take on a mind of its own without the constraints of tradition and rote) and the desire to multiply and divide into more groups.

I am not advocating the cell church organization, but the direction back to New Testament principles of gathering exhibited in many of these churches is exciting. The church is becoming reachable and spiritually tangible again among God's people who compose it. The church was intended to be in the hands of the common people—not controlled by clergy, or manipulated by those with high theological degrees or enslaved by denomination structures.

Similar to the cell church structure, many of the New Testament churches met in homes and were small in size.

The New Testament church meetings were simple, but ordered and scheduled. For example, they met at least weekly at an arranged time for the breaking of the bread and for teaching (Acts 20:7).

Those in New Testament churches were active in reaching the lost for Christ and discipling new converts in the teachings of Christ (Mt. 28:18-20). Paul acknowledges the great dissemination of truth in that first thirty years of the church age after Pentecost (Col. 1:6, 23). It should be a normal practice of every church gathering to continue reaching new areas of the community with God's truth and love. Maintaining the New Testament practice of spreading truth will usually require a growing church to hive off, seeing new gatherings beginning in other parts of the community. However, much focus today is on achieving big church status, with big church buildings. Almost inevitably, this creates big church problems—problems that small churches normally don't have to contemplate.

For example, small gatherings of Christians don't have parking problems or need multiple teaching services to divide up the flock. With a small gathering of Christians, it is easy to discern who is missing (often known beforehand). Sitting in close proximity generally eliminates a need for sound and light systems. Renting a room for the meetings or meeting in the home doesn't tie up the Lord's money in bricks and mortar and in maintenance, utility, and cleaning costs. Small groups allow everyone to intimately know everyone else, so there is a sense of oneness, mutual support and accountability. A small meeting promotes participation by everyone in the work, thus spiritual gifts are developed. A small group is easier to shepherd and provides a conducive environment for understanding who God has raised up as part of the plural spiritual oversight (Acts

20:28). This is the biblical pattern of the New Testament church.

The following true story illustrates the problem of many churches today. It was relayed to me by a brother in the Lord from Louisiana named Bob. He has a friend who is senior pastor of a 1500-member evangelical church in that state. Not having his friend's phone number handy, Bob went to the phone book to look it up. He discovered that his friend had an unlisted number. Later, when the two were able to visit, Bob confronted the pastor about how God's sheep would be able to reach him during difficult times with an unlisted number. The man's response was, "Do you know how many calls I would get if I had a listed telephone number?" Bob's response was, "Not many if your church were fifteen churches of a hundred people with ten elders overseeing and pastoring each church."

Although it is exciting to see the cell churches reassert some New Testament basics, many hindrances to regaining the blessings of a true New Testament church meeting still remain. For most, a denominational or church structure still forbids local cell autonomy. Clergy and/or other salaried employees usually retain control of the cell groups instead of a plurality of godly men. Or in other groups the danger of congregational democracy occurs (the people rule). A lack of church order is prevalent, and appropriate biblical gender roles/ministries within the group are often not followed. But, despite these areas needing growth, the general movement toward scriptural simplicity by many cell churches is thrilling.

History has shown that, as governments persecute their subjects, the New Testament pattern for gathering emerges again. In present-day Communist and Muslim states there are thousands of home church meetings convened each week according to the New Testament pattern. It is the only way they can meet. Perhaps, the continued moral demise and anti-Christian agenda of our society will play a major role in returning Christians to biblical Christianity! So, don't be surprised if the Lord blesses your outreach study in such a way that a new church begins meeting in your very own living room. It has happened before, and it will happen again!

2

Christ's Touch

The Lord was superb at drawing sinners to Himself. Why was He so effective in reaching the unsaved? Let's think together about the following passage.

Then He went out again by the sea; and all the multitude came to Him, and He taught them. And as He passed by, He saw Levi the son of Alphaeus sitting at the tax office, and He said to him, "Follow Me." And he arose and followed Him. Now it happened, as He was dining in Levi's house, that many tax collectors and sinners also sat together with Jesus and His disciples; for there were many, and they followed Him. And when the scribes and Pharisees saw Him eating with the tax collectors and sinners, they said to His disciples, "How is it that He eats and drinks with tax collectors and sinners?" When Jesus heard it, He said to them, "Those who are well have no need of a physician, but those who are sick. I did not come to call the righteous, but sinners, to repentance" (Mk. 2:13-17, NKJV).

Our Lord called Levi (better known as Matthew) into joyful fellowship. In appreciation, Levi invited his friends (other sinners, publicans and IRS associates) to a feast in his home. The Lord was rubbing shoulders with a household of sinful people. The Son of God Himself was creating personal connections with the sinners He came to save. It was a beautiful scene of God's love, only slightly spoiled by religious leaders who concluded Jesus was a sinner because He associated with sinners—a mistake many Christians make today!

But the Lord clearly explained to these browbeating Pharisees that He was a physician. He had come to heal the sick, and a physician must spend time with the sick to achieve this goal. The Lord was and is the great Physician! Like any good physician, He hated the disease that was killing His patients, but didn't transfer His anger about the matter to the patient. Don't we expect the same from our family doctor? Would you expect your doctor to verbally abuse you about a congenital disease you have, perhaps a disease you have suffered with all your life? Or, would you expect your doctor to show a bit of compassion, fostered in honest dialogue? All men are born with a congenital condition called "sin" that plagues us throughout life and if not cured will eventually hurl us into an endless agony apart from God. In this case, the cure and the Physician were one, and both were within the grasp of the hurting and spiritually sick.

Those conducting home outreach Bible studies must have the same kind of tender compassion that the Lord had for the lost. God hates sin, but loves the sinner. We, too, should love the sinner and hate sin. We should mimic the Great Physician by seeking to cure the disease called sin and not just treating its symptoms. Try your best to look beyond the cigarette smoke, the foul language, and the crude remarks to an eternal soul that is afflicted and urgently needs the Lord. As with a physical disease, you will not be able to see improvement of the symptoms of sin until there is progress resolving the main problem—the hardened heart.

A few years ago, the Lord glorified Himself by saving a fellow aerospace engineer through a one-on-one work place Bible study. This man's language was often crude and sometimes vulgar. Except for the instances when he took the Lord's name in vain, I said nothing. We met together four times before he acknowledged Jesus Christ as Saviour, then we continued meeting for several months of discipleship. I prayed that the Holy Spirit would convict this man about his unruly speech, and one day during a study, the Lord answered that prayer. The man told me that the Lord had been showing him that he needed to clean up his mouth. I said, "You're right. Your language is terrible, and now that the Lord has shown you that from His Word, I will help keep you accountable." It only took a few weeks for a noticeable change to occur, and a few more months for this sin symptom to disappear. The Lord healed him of this consequence of sin.

I might note that there are methods to reprove an unsaved person of taking the Lord's name in vain without creating undo tension between you. Perhaps you might ask, "Were you praying to God just then or using His name in vain?" He will usually get the point. If he doesn't, explain that the Lord Jesus is very precious to you and that you would prefer him not to vainly use His name while you are studying together. You can also explain that this is the third of the Ten Commandments (Ex. 20:7).

Howard Hendricks tells of his first experience in a home Bible study while he was a seminary student:

A host invited me to visit a study session in his home. I gladly accepted the invitation. So when I got to the home and knocked on the door, the host answered and I asked, "Is this where the Bible class meets?" Just then I saw the place was filled with smoke. I apologized, "Oh, I'm awfully sorry; I'm at the wrong place." The host replied, "Aren't you Mr. Hendricks? We're expecting you. This is the Bible class. Come on in." I still remember walking into the smoke-filled room. For the first time I realized that letting non-Christians smoke was no barrier to their studying the Bible! On the contrary, if a host or hostess says to prospective class members, "You can't smoke here," most if not all of them would respond, "Then we won't come."

He later notes that after they receive Christ as Saviour, nearly all the smokers drop the cigarette habit.

We were confronted with the same situation in an outreach study a few years ago. Our next-door neighbor, John (a chain smoker), came to a small Bible study in our home. Because of our own children and other children who were in my wife's class, we preferred that there be no smoking in the house. It might drive away non-smoking attendees. Our solution was to take a short break midway through the study for refreshments. This allowed John to go outside (often accompanied by me) to smoke a cigarette. We would then return and enjoy our refreshments together while finishing up the study. Several thousand cigarettes later (eight month's worth), John repented of his sins and professed Christ as Saviour.

The Lord did not hesitate to be involved with sinners and make lasting connections with them despite their bad habits (symptoms). One of the problems of our day is that too few Christians work at maintaining friendships with the unsaved. This is the best way to see an evangelistic outreach Bible study begin. Some have interpreted personal holiness as not being defiled with sinners instead of not being defiled by sin. Many Christians feel they will be contaminated by sin if they spend too much time with non-believers. The solution is to find ways of building relationships in areas of life where the Christian does not have to compromise his convictions or lower the holy standard for living that God decrees.

For example, go out to lunch with an unsaved co-worker (of like gender) who is struggling in his marriage. Ladies, have that frazzled mother with out-of-control tots over for tea and a heartstring-tying visit. Have that unsaved family, that your children have made connections with, over for dinner. Perhaps a back-to-school or watermelon party in your yard will provide an opportunity to meet your neighbors. You don't have to go into taverns and casinos to connect with the hoards of hell-bound suffering people in the world. Just be available and listen.

Work to establish connections and show the love of Christ through the opportunities God gives. As Paul confirms to the saints at Corinth, *"God...maketh manifest the savour of His knowledge by us in every place"* (2 Cor. 2:14). When we live Christ, the world breathes in afresh the sweetness of the Saviour. We become reflectors of light and grace from the Son to a dark world. The aroma of Christlikeness is an invigorating fragrance in the world. It will tantalize and constrain even the hardest hearts to stop and savor a divine expression of love.

"Jesus came and touched them, and said, Arise, and be not afraid. And when they had lifted up their eyes, they saw no man, except Jesus only" (Mt. 17:7-8).

What do a leper, four blind men, and three disciples have in common? They were all touched by Christ to satisfy a deep longing. The leper was a social outcast and desired to be embraced, to have the caring touch of another person.

21

For the blind, every clumsy step ventured into the unknown, but the Lord lifted this darkness and gave their souls security. The fearful disciples were comforted in a time of panic. Why didn't the Lord just speak a good word? He understood that a loving touch could convey what words couldn't. There are many hurting, blind, and afraid people who need the Saviour's touch today. Let us not fear to reach out and touch those in need, so they too might see no one but Jesus!

> *Let my hands perform His bidding,*
> *Let my feet run in His ways,*
> *Let my eyes see Jesus only,*
> *Let my lips speak forth His praise.*
> —MARY D. JAMES

3

Making Disciples through Evangelistic Studies

Perhaps the best place to begin talking about biblical evangelistic techniques is with our personal responsibility to evangelize. Note the Lord's words to the eleven disciples after His resurrection, just prior to His ascension into heaven: *"All power is given unto Me in heaven and in earth. Go ye therefore, and teach all nations, baptizing them in the name of the Father, and of the Son, and of the Holy Ghost: Teaching them to observe all things whatsoever I have commanded you: and, lo, I am with you alway, even unto the end of the world. Amen"* (Mt. 28:18-20).

Notice the four "alls" in this passage. *"All"* authority was given to Christ; the disciples were to go to *"all"* nations, teaching *"all"* things Christ taught them and that He would be with them *"always."* The fact that this was a propagating command from disciple to disciple is evident in that eleven men could not possibly reach the whole world, teaching all things until the end of the Church Age. In this passage, the Lord reveals His master plan in growing His Church—making disciples. "Disciple" comes from the Greek word *mathētēs*, which means a learner (not just a follower). According to Matthew 11:29 and 10:25, the disciple of Christ is not learning a trade, but a person—Christ—and desires to become like Him.

What does it mean to be a disciple of Christ? Not much in modern Christianity, unfortunately, but the biblical answer to this question is very relevant in leading evangelistic studies and then discipling new converts. The teacher must tell those who are young in the Lord the cost of being a disciple of Christ. Christ did! He gave a gospel message (kingdom message) then immediately followed the invitation with a discipleship declaration (Mk. 1; Lk. 4, 9, 14).

I usually tell new converts within a few weeks of their conversion to use every connection they have with the unsaved because within a year they will likely lose most, if not all, their close friendships with non-Christians. Commonality is essential to maintain friendships, and much of what binds people together today is not godly. So, new converts must utilize fading friendships to share their faith. If possible, they should be encouraged to maintain as many of these connections as possible without compromising their testimony.

One young Christian relayed to me the words of his next door neighbor a few months after his conversion: "We like you guys a lot, but we don't want to talk about religious stuff any more. So, if you promise not to do that, then we can be friends. Otherwise, we would rather not see you anymore." Consequently, this friendship quickly faded.

The concept of discipleship is mentioned 264 times in the four Gospel accounts and the book of Acts. There is no doubt it was heavy on the Lord's heart. It is evident from Luke 14 that the Lord was not interested in quantity, but quality. He didn't merely want obedient followers; He wanted committed disciples. Obedience can be forced, but submission is a heart issue—it is a matter of the will. It is not a matter of Christ being in your heart, but does He have your heart? Being in fellowship with God is dependent on giving Him your will. Active submission is the key to being a disciple.

Notice the passages where the Lords pleads with us to be His disciples.

1. *"If any man come to Me, and hate not his father, and mother, and wife, and children, and brethren and sisters, yea and his own life also, he cannot be My disciple"* (Lk. 14:26). From the parallel account in Matthew 10:34-39, we understand that the word "hate" is a comparative term. Our love for the Lord should be so much greater than any natural affection we might have for another, that comparatively it would seem like hate.

2. *"And whosoever doth not bear his cross, and come after Me, cannot be My disciple"* (Lk. 14:27). The cross was a symbol of shame, reproach, and death. Christ suffered these for us; now He asks the believer to suffer for Him (though not for the purpose of His death, of course).

3. *"So likewise, whosoever he be of you that forsaketh not all that he hath, he cannot be my disciple"* (Lk. 14:33).

4. *"It is enough for the disciple that he be as his master, and the servant as his lord"* (Mt. 10:25).

5. *"Come unto Me, all ye that labor and are heavy laden, and I will give you rest. Take My yoke upon you, and learn of Me; for I am meek and lowly in heart, and ye shall find rest unto your souls. For My yoke is easy, and My burden light"* (Mt. 11:28-30).

6. Summarized in Luke 9:23, *"If any man will come after Me, let him deny himself and take up his cross daily,*

and follow Me. For whosoever will save his life shall lose it; but whosoever will lose his life for My sake, the same shall save it."

A "disciple" is a title given to those actively pursuing Christ and forsaking the "fluff" of life. A disciple desires to be like Christ. It is not enough to be a Christ-one (a Christian); one must seek to be Christ-like. It is not enough to go to the cross for salvation; we must leave Calvary with a cross of our own. It is not enough to come to Christ; we must go on with Him. He was born to die; the Christian has been born again to live for Christ and die to self. If you are discipling new converts, this aspect of Lordship must be at the center of everything taught about Christianity.

Christ would grow the church by making disciples, who would go out and make more disciples. I praise God for evangelistic outreach events (i.e., stadium crusades, tent meetings, etc.), but the vast majority of people won to Christ are through the one-on-one efforts of individuals and not big productions. Evangelist Bill Fay estimates only about fifteen percent of people professing Christ as Saviour are saved through evangelistic events.

I praise God for evangelists, but they were never intended by God to save the world. One important aspect of the evangelist's work is to equip the church to evangelize (Eph. 4:11-12). Yes, as part of that encouragement and perfecting of the church, they do lead others to the truth, but their main calling is to stir up the rest of us to live and preach Christ. We need to preach Christ everywhere by our lives, and then, when appropriate, use words to explain what has already been witnessed within us.

Is it statistically possible to win the world population of 6 billion to Christ through the Lord's discipleship plan?

Although some have placed the present "professing"

Christian population at 2 billion, perhaps 1.5 billion is a bit more realistic estimate. Of these professing Christians, I will assume that only 1 in 15 are actually trusting in Christ alone for salvation and have been truly regenerated by the Holy Spirit. We will assume 100,000,000 spiritually alive, born-again individuals are walking planet Earth today.

Let us also assume that every true Christian sees one person come to Christ each year and disciples that new convert for one year. Then both the new covert and the original discipler lead someone to Christ again the next year, and this process repeats every year. We will also assume for this analysis that there is a 2.5 percent mortality rate of Christians and a 4.0 percent world population growth rate. What would the outcome be after each year?

Year 1	Year 2	Year 3	Year 4	Year 5	Year 6	Year 7
Number of Believers (in billions)						
0.198	0.390	0.770	1.521	3.005	5.935	11.721
World Population (in billions)						
6.240	6.490	6.749	7.019	7.300	7.592	7.896

What is the conclusion? Although we know that not everyone will repent of their sins and acknowledge Christ as Saviour, the Lord's plan of growing the church through discipleship is "do-able." The greatest hindrance to church growth is not communism or liberals undermining the Word of God or humanists teaching evolution and new age propaganda in government schools. The greatest threat to the spread of Christianity is that blood-bought, born-again Christians are not being disciples of Jesus Christ.

We are chickens! We let our fear threaten our desire to please the Lord! Perhaps we worry about what others will think, whether we have enough knowledge, or that we will lose business opportunities. What God thinks should be our only consideration. If you're saved, you have enough knowledge to present the gospel. The Lord clearly answers the last question, *"For whosoever will save his life shall lose it; but whosoever will lose his life for My sake, the same shall save it"* (Lk. 9:24).

The wonderful thing about God is that He loves to use cowards. Moses and Gideon are good examples. By using the least likely people to accomplish His will, He brings the greater glory to Himself and assures no flesh will glory in His presence (1 Cor. 1:26-29). If you are a willing chicken, you are exactly who God wants to use!

Start by focusing your prayers, attention, and energy on just one unsaved person. Many of my outreach study opportunities have been with one person. Of these, there is a high conversion rate compared to a larger-sized study (which makes it easier for folks to slide out of it). Don't be discouraged about only one or two people coming to your home for a study, or meeting with one unsaved co-worker at noon. Just do it!

My wife was exercised to lead a one evening evangelistic outreach study in the home of a new convert named Carrie. Carrie had been saved less than a month. She was a social butterfly and had scores of unsaved friends. She was also extremely excited about inviting her unsaved friends to this study and proceeded to invite over sixty women! The evening of the study, Carrie was very disappointed at the number of women who actually came. She had worked so hard and felt that a study of twenty-two women was a flop. I remember smiling at my wife as she told me Carrie's disappointment. In my mind, I drifted back to times when we had no one show up to an outreach study (which then became a prayer meeting). If you get twenty-two souls in your home to hear the gospel, be sure to tell the Lord an emphatic "Thank You!" You may have invited the people, but He brought them.

I believe that we are living in the final hours of the Church Age and in the days of "hand-picked fruit," not highly mechanized mass production methods. Let us be disciples of Christ and seek to make the same—one soul at a time. Success in evangelism is sharing your faith with others. Only God can bless the seeds you have planted and bring the increase. It has been my observation that the small group evangelistic Bible study has been the single most effective tool in sowing the gospel seed into the hearts of men. Sowing seed is success on our part; God is the One responsible for the results (1 Cor. 3:6).

4

Using Biblical Evangelistic Techniques in Your Studies

How is the love of God communicated to an unsaved person—without driving them away? The best answer to this question can be found in studying how the Lord and the Apostles mingled, connected, and communicated with needy souls. Let's quickly explore five such engagements. This will generate some practical evangelistic techniques for communicating to the lost. Since these are conversations of a wide range of people (a hiding adulterous woman, a seeking blue-collar worker, a politician, the religious zealot, and a mocking lawyer), surely at least one encounter will fit the individual you have in mind.

THE SAMARITAN WOMAN AT THE WELL (JN. 4)

The Lord began His conversation by making a parallel connection between her physical need (water) and her spiritual void (her soul's need of Himself). After creating a simple analogy, which the woman understood, the Lord gets to a key issue often forfeited today in gospel outreach:

31

sin. He confronted her with her sin. Notice He didn't start the conversation with, "You're a sinner going to hell!" or "If you died today..." The Lord doesn't talk about dying; He talks to her about living the abundant life. However, that cannot happen without understanding what inhibits us from living that life and what separates us from God. The Lord didn't skirt the matter of sin. He compassionately exposed it and answered her question—which was her attempt to get the conversation off herself and onto religious bypaths. The Lord used the question to refocus her attention back to what really matters—a relationship with Himself, the awaited Messiah.

Before we can see people saved, we have to ensure they know they are lost. A man with a pride-inflated life jacket doesn't feel the need of a Saviour, but a man who knows he is being pulled under by the heavy weight of his sin will cry out to be saved.

How successful was the Lord? She came with a water pot to draw water, but left it at the well to draw men to Christ. What was important to her before she met the Saviour was not so important afterwards. These are two signs of true faith and of being a disciple of Christ. Forsaking to following Him leads to pointing others to Him as well.

Use spiritual illustrations to teach the concept of grace versus earning salvation by good works. Grace is unmerited favor or **G**od's **R**iches **A**t **C**hrist's **E**xpense. This can be done by holding up a prize and telling the listener that there is nothing he or she can do to earn this prize, but it is for whoever will come and receive it as a gift. Or, perhaps tell someone you want to trade him or her your new, expensive ink pen for their old, cheap, plastic one. The individual may try to pay you for it or give you something else for it.

However, you explain it is a gift that must be received; it cannot be paid for. Then, don't miss the opportunity of explaining that God pays a fair wage for sin. It is called death (Rom. 6:23; 4:4). Death in the Bible means eternal separation from God in a place called hell. God does not desire that they go there, and He will give the free gift of eternal life to those who accept it. If they respond and believe this message, their sins will be forgiven and their conscience will be cleared of guilt (Heb. 9:9).

PHILIP AND ETHIOPIAN EUNUCH (ACTS 8)

Notice in verse 29 that Philip was attentive to the Holy Spirit's leading. This is so important. To my shame, I acknowledge that there have been times when I sensed the Spirit's prompting to talk to someone, but because of one reason or another, I didn't obey. The more you grow in the Lord, the more obvious His leading is.

I remember driving with my family on a 600-mile road trip to visit my wife's family. At that time, Brenda and I had three children under the age of six. Halfway through the trip, we stopped at a fast food restaurant to eat. I went to order food, while my wife corralled the children into the restroom. The young woman who took my order had shoulder-length blonde hair, hollow blue eyes, and a fallen countenance. I don't know what her situation was, but I could feel her pain over the counter. I was feeling burdened to say a kind word and hand her a tract, but I didn't. We ate our meal and my wife started loading the children back into the van. I was feeling convicted about not obeying the Lord, but I rationalized, "I'm on an eleven-hour road trip with the family; the Lord understands."

Returning to our vehicle, I noticed someone sitting on the sidewalk smoking a cigarette with her head hung down.

Yes, you guessed it. The Lord was giving me a second chance. As I climbed into our van, my wife said, "I think we should give this woman a gospel tract before we leave." The Lord was now using my own wife to get the point across. For a moment, I pondered the situation. It was enough time for the flesh to rationalize the opportunity away. I was a man on a mission; it just wasn't the Great Commission. I thought about how tired and cranky the children were getting. I thought about the loss of sleep resulting from arriving in the early morning hours. I started the van and drove away.

Little did I know that the experience would ruin my trip and haunt my conscience for several years. I learned from that lesson to follow the Spirit's prompting. If you are not willing to do the Lord's bidding, He will find someone else to do it; then they will get the reward that could have been yours. This is the lesson Elijah learned after slipping into spiritual depression (1 Ki. 19) and it reflects the exhortation by the Lord to the church of Philadelphia, *"Hold that fast which thou hast, that no man take thy crown"* (see Rev. 3:11). This was the victor's crown. It was bestowed on the winner of a sporting contest, and is generally used in the New Testament to speak of reward given to properly motivated Christians for faithful service. In my case, I am sad to have lost the reward, but I do pray that someone else was used by God to reach this woman and got the reward.

Secondly, Philip was willing to venture down into the desert to reach one lost soul for Christ. Did someone go the extra mile to see you saved? Perhaps one burdened individual fervently prayed for years for you to come to Christ. Maybe a friend patiently took your repeated insults after sharing God's truth with you. Go the extra mile to see others saved; don't give up easily. Perhaps someone doesn't call you when they are supposed to, or they stand you up for a meeting. Don't get irritated! This is a spiritual battle for an eternal soul. Expect some setbacks and frustrations.

Thirdly, Philip didn't give the Eunuch a rehearsed speech or Sunday's sermon notes. Philip just started where the Lord was already enlightening the Eunuch in the Scriptures (Isa. 53). From that point, he *"preached unto him Jesus"* (Acts 8:35). After explaining that Jesus was the fulfillment of the passage he had been studying, Philip brought the conversation to a close. What will it be? Help them make a decision. Christians often ignore this step because it can be uncomfortable, usually because high-pressure tactics or self-righteous attitudes are present. If people sense your love and concern for them, this will not be a stressful step. God doesn't use high-pressure tactics to force people into repentance; neither should we.

Recently, a man remained behind after a noontime workplace Bible study. He was from a religious background and was just starting to understand the gift of God's grace through Christ versus working one's way to heaven. Under deep conviction, he commented, "I wish I had never come to this study. I wish I didn't know what I know now."

I made direct eye contact with him, and said, "Mark, listen to this verse," and I quoted John 3:18 to him. "There was a time when you could claim ignorance and ignorantly go to hell, but now you know the truth and, in your heart, you have already made a decision. You cannot ride the fence with Jesus. You either believe Him or call Him a liar. He will force no one into heaven. The choice is yours; what will it be?"

Before the next study, Mark had trusted Christ as his Saviour! Later that year, his son also put his faith in the Lord Jesus. A dad impacted by the gospel often leads to a

35

family changed forever.

PAUL BEFORE FESTUS, AGRIPPA, AND BERNICE (ACTS 26)

Paul shared his personal testimony with these political aristocrats. His testimony was full of facts, which gives evidence of the truth. Pursuing detail is a means of determining the truth.

This is a technique I enjoy employing with my children when I receive multiple conflicting stories for one incident. If you get them talking long enough, eventually the error will be found out. State the truth always, and truth will state consistent detail. If you always tell the truth, you need not be concerned about conflicting statements. Paul's testimony was bathed in Old Testament scriptures to prick the ears of his Jewish audience. He clearly reviewed his life before Christ, how he became a Christian, and how Christ was presently using him.

When accused of being mad, Paul simply stated, "I just speak words of truth." We need not apologize for the truth spoken in love (Eph. 4:15). The gospel is offensive and foolish to the lost (1 Cor. 1:18), but we don't have to be foolish or offensive in sharing the gospel. The best way to defuse an intense situation is the path of humility. If you sacrifice yourself and take the low place, normally the ego of the other is satisfied with the high place and will cease the verbal onslaught.

Sometimes folks in outreach or new convert discipleship studies get the notion that the teacher is flawless. It is important that teachers dispel this by being honest with those they are discipling. Reveal past personal failures or human errors during studies. Christ must increase, and we must decrease. Godly men and women never draw others to themselves, but point others to Christ. Don't try to build yourself up in the Bible studies, or you will eventually lose your audience.

PETER ADDRESSES A JEWISH CROWD ON PENTECOST (ACTS 2)

The baptism of the Holy Spirit on the disciples of Christ brought confusion, amazement and fear to onlookers at Pentecost. At least ten distinct foreign languages were heard proclaiming the gospel message. Some thought these Christians were drunk. What was Peter's defense to this accusation? He simply quoted God's Word, using the Scriptures to clarify the events taking place. Speaking to a mainly Jewish audience, he wisely used Old Testament passages to teach about Christ's person, death, resurrection, and present position. He then boldly proclaimed the necessity of repentance to receive forgiveness of sins through Jesus the Messiah (Acts 2:28). The Word of God revealing Christ to the hearer should be central to evangelism: *"Faith cometh by hearing, and hearing by the Word of God"* (Rom. 10:17).

One of the most fruitful techniques of evangelism is to move your guests through a list of questions until you have them reading the Word of God. I have never had anyone end a spiritual conversation after they read the Word of God aloud. It is an amazing thing to see nervous souls explore the Bible for the first time, being deeply moved as discoveries of truth are made. What a privilege to be an observer of divine grace in action!

I have found the best way to explain the gospel is to ask basic questions and have the unsaved person read Scripture aloud to determine the answer for themselves. Of course, this is accomplished through the working of the Holy Spirit. Only He can enlighten and convict (Jn. 16:7-11). If you don't get a clear answer, have them read the verse again aloud, but don't try to bridge the gap for them. Don't cheat them out of the discovery experience of seeing truth for themselves! If they don't understand, have them read a parallel passage, and ask the same question again, perhaps worded slightly differently. Every time they read a passage of Scripture, the power of God's Word and Spirit are being unleashed on the unregenerate soul before your eyes!

JESUS AND A LAWYER (LK. 10:25-29)
JESUS AND THE ELDERS (MT. 21:23-25)

The Lord employed two techniques with these hard-hearted people. With the lawyer, He answered his question with a question and by that referred to Scripture. The lawyer was not interested in being saved, but sought to test the Lord. He hoped to outwit God through a question about obtaining salvation. What a fool! Although this blind lawyer's motives were poor, the Lord graciously provided him an opportunity to see the truth with two questions: "What does the Scripture say?" and "What does the Scripture say to you?" Note that the lawyer was the one quoting Scripture. These are great questions to help us move out of difficult situations, especially when talking to someone with a lawyer type of personality. You put the burden back on them to declare the truth. It is very difficult to get into an argument if you simply ask the inquirer to read Scripture and then ask, "What does that verse say to you?"

With the Jewish elders, Jesus provided an illustration to answer their question. It illustrates the adage, "A picture is worth a thousand words." The Lord used many word pictures in the forms of metaphors, allegories, parables and illustrations to explain spiritual truth. Don't underestimate the benefit of a clear illustration, a drawing, a time line, a chart, a table, or a story to help inquirers see the truth.

In summary, the six evangelistic techniques derived from the above five passages are:

1. The need and means of salvation must be revealed from Scripture (sin, repentance, the cross).

2. Use your personal testimony to validate the truth of the gospel to the hearer.

3. Present the gospel from the hearer's vantage point via the connection you have made with them.

4. Use simple questions and the reading of God's Word aloud to avoid personal conflict.

5. Use illustrations to explain spiritual truths.

6. Bring the discussion to a low-pressure invitation at the conclusion. "What do you think of Christ?"

5

The Study Leader

Many Christians, even some infants in the Lord, desire to be Bible study leaders. Perhaps they were saved through a small group study, and for this reason this method seems to them to be the best. Zealousness for the Lord or a burden for the lost may carry some from personal evangelism into leading evangelistic studies before they have a scriptural foundation or an understanding of their spiritual exercise and abilities. Often, this situation will do more harm than good in reaching the lost. I call it "the toppled tree scenario." A young Christian tries to branch out to others before he is sufficiently rooted in the Lord to sustain the weight. There is a need to *"take root downward"* before we *"bear fruit upward"* (Isa. 37:31). Without a certain amount of experience and wisdom from God, the tree topples.

Although all Christians are to be evangelical, not all Christians are intended by God to lead evangelical Bible studies. It takes a person that God has prepared and called especially for this ministry. This is true of any God-ordained ministry. The sovereign God designs all sorts of vessels for service in His house (2 Tim. 2:20-21). The same is true in our own homes where we have hundreds of gadgets and tools for specific purposes. Wouldn't your neigh-bor think you a bit strange if he saw you trying to open a can of soup with a rolling pin, or cleaning potatoes with a cheese grater? I wonder what God thinks as He watches Christians engaging in spiritual activities without the right spiritual tools.

You may be asking yourself the question, "Am I cut out to lead Bible studies?" Let me suggest to you three pre-requisites for teaching a small group Bible study. If you meet these three prerequisites, prayerfully consider moving ahead in this ministry. Since the general purpose of spiritu-al gifts is to build up the church (Eph. 4:12; 1 Pet. 4:10) or in some cases to reach the lost with the gospel (Acts 2:7-13; 1 Cor. 14:22), an evaluation of your efforts in accom-plishing these purposes is necessary. Is your ministry bene-fiting the church? If you see God blessing your labor, then keep on keeping on!

It should be firmly stated that every believer has a responsibility to let the light of Christ shine and to be a witness for the Lord Jesus. It may be that you are not designed to lead evangelistic Bible studies, but this does not excuse you from personal evangelism. If you are saved, you know enough to lead someone else to the Lord. Peter exhorts, *"But sanctify the Lord God in your hearts, and be ready always to give an answer to every man that asketh you a reason of the hope that is in you with meekness and fear"* (1 Pet. 3:15).

The first prerequisite for leading a Bible study is a teaching gift which is applicable to a small group format. Paul informs us of the specific nature of spiritual gifts bestowed by the Holy Spirit in 1 Corinthians 12:4-6, 11. For example, these gifts will vary in diversity (number), administration (the manner used), and operation (to whom ministered). Just because you have the spiritual gift of teaching, it doesn't mean you are well-equipped to lead a Bible study. Even if you are divinely called to lead studies, it is best, if possible, to be mentored for a while (sit in on a study with a veteran leader at the helm) as an aid to developing your gift. It is best if we understand group dynamics, the accountability to God in teaching, and how to teach God's Word before attempting this ministry. Leading a small group study requires having some teaching ability balanced with tender leadership skills (having a shepherd's heart and staff).

It has been my observation that generally preachers and lecturers make poor small group leaders. On the contrary, most small group leaders aren't exceptional in pulpits. God planned it out that way, so we would learn to depend on each other and learn how to love each other in using our gifts and abilities for the cause of Christ.

Moody Monthly magazine explains this reality:

> To oversimplify, a discussion leader may be either too strong or too weak. The strong type is a better lecturer. Discussion to him is having his questions answered "correctly." His questions are specific— sometimes only requiring a yes or no answer.
>
> If he is too weak, his discussion is probably characterized by indirection. He starts with a question and lets someone else take it from there. Group members get side-tracked on borderline matters or heated arguments.[1]

The second criterion for leading a small group Bible study is spiritual exercise and excitement in doing so. Is God burdening your heart for this ministry? Do you feel God has placed you in this particular environment at this time for the purpose of reaching workmates, neighbors, family members, etc? Do you have a heart that beats for the lost? Will you be willing to sacrifice time with family, damage to your house, and exposure to sinful attitudes and behaviors in order to reach these unsaved folks? As Howard Hendricks has said, "When God takes His tape measure to you, He'll measure your heart, not your head!" If you don't have a compassionate heart for lonely, hurting hell-bound sinners, don't start a Bible study.

Are you excited about the study? Excitement is contagious. George Whitefield preached all over Britain in the 18th century. One morning, he was preaching in a little chapel in Scotland. The meeting began at 6:00 AM (before daylight), and people from all over the area were streaming into the church building. The town skeptic was seen walking towards the chapel, and a passerby yelled out at him, "I didn't think you believe in such things." The skeptic replied "I don't, but he does and I can't stay away."

There is something about sincerity and excitement which is contagious. If you are excited about discovering the unfathomed depths of God's Word, others will grow in excitement, too.

The final prerequisite is to have a fundamental knowledge of Bible doctrine and to be living it. You don't have to have seminary degrees or Bible college courses under your belt to teach the Bible. Having a good overview of Scripture (with relevant historical information), an understanding of basic doctrines, and the knowledge of how to use study tools will go far in leading a study. The teacher will learn more by teaching than any attendee will by attending the group.

There are two great spiritual by-products of leading a group study: the teacher learns as he ministers, and the study provides accountability to be in God's Word regularly and systematically.

The second aspect of knowing sound doctrine is living sound doctrine (Titus 2:1). If your testimony doesn't agree with what you will be teaching, then learn it yourself first (Lk. 6:39-44)! Then teach others what is proper doctrine.

Albert Wollen emphasizes the importance of the spiritual life of the study leader in his book, *How to Conduct Home Study Classes.* He writes:

> The leader of the home Bible study is the most vital member of the class. Obviously, his spiritual life is of great importance. Unless he has a vital and close relationship with Christ, there is little likelihood the class will be able to grow spiritually. The Holy Spirit will be hindered if the leader is spiritually indifferent or troubled with unconfessed sin. A person not free to the working of the Holy Spirit in his own life can hardly be a channel for His working in the group.[2]

How important did the Apostle Paul think teaching sound doctrine was in training God's people? Listen to his counsel to Timothy and Titus (his younger trainees in pastoral care).

I. Exhortation to Timothy:
   a. Preserve sound doctrine (1 Tim. 1:3)
   b. Reprove, rebuke, exhort with all long suffering and doctrine (2 Tim. 4:2)
   c. Study to show thyself approved (2 Tim. 2:15)
II. Exhortation to Titus:
   a. Those leading must, by sound doctrine, exhort and confront the opposers (Titus 1:9)
   b. But speak thou the things which become sound doctrine (Titus 2:1)

Paul had a passion for the Word of God, and so should any Bible teacher. He understood that the Word of God sharpens our conscience to what is right and wrong. Without understanding sound doctrine, we will not be able to lead others into discerning right and wrong. The teacher himself will not be able to spot error when it is blatantly hurled in front of the entire group. Paul never lost his passion for God's Word. Just shortly before being put to death, Paul instructed Timothy to bring the Word of God with him when he came to visit Paul in prison (2 Tim. 4:13). A teacher must have a passion for the Word of God!

Do you have spiritual exercise and the appropriate gift and know and live sound doctrine? If so, pray to the Lord to prepare the hearts of potential attendees to receive first the invitation and then receive the good seed. Set a date, invite and invite and wait to see whom the Spirit of God brings. You will soon find out if the Lord is in it or not.

6

Inviting Others and Getting Started

How do you get started? First of all, what is it that you feel the Lord is calling you to do? What is your spiritual exercise? Perhaps a one-on-one study with an unsaved person or a larger outreach study or a discipleship study? Most evangelistic studies will begin small in numbers (perhaps just with one person) in response to an opportunity that God has provided. Often, these small studies grow into larger ones.

The following true story is given as an example of making a connection with a searching soul and seeing an evangelistic study start. About four years ago, I arrived at work at 7:00 AM to ensure I had a full hour lunch break for a Bible study I was teaching at the place where I was employed at the time. I laid my Bible on my desk and walked up to the coffee center for my first cup of morning brew. Another man, named Craig, whom I only knew remotely, was just a few steps behind me. After exchanging a "Good morning," I poured him a cup of coffee, then proceeded to fill my own mug. I wasn't expecting any more conversation at that time in the morning, but he broke the silence with the question, "Is that a Bible on your desk?"

"Yes, it sure is," was my response.

After another moment of stillness, Craig asked, "Do you read it?"

Glancing up briefly, I said, "Yes, Craig, normally I read it every day." There was more silence. Trying to act as casually as possible, I simply asked him, "Do you have a Bible?"

He quickly responded, "Yes."

"Do you read it?"

He hesitated in responding, then, looking down at his coffee mug, said, "Well, I use to, but I don't any more."

I told Craig that what he needed was accountability, and if he would give me thirteen lunch hours, I would teach him the main points of the Bible.

He responded with a smile, "Really, man, in just thirteen lessons I'll understand what the Bible is about?"

I told him that this would be the case if he would faithfully invest time in studying the Bible and in coming to our weekly noon study with his homework finished. Although he stood me up twice and we had to move the study to 6:30 in the morning to accommodate his schedule, Craig came to know the Saviour between our third and fourth study together. Three months later, his wife was saved, and later, his oldest son professed Jesus Christ as Saviour. They are now a pillar family in our local assembly.

Pray for connections, then when God provides them, seize the moment and be as kind and flexible as possible.

Although many outreach studies will begin with just one person, you may be sensing the Lord burdening your heart about a specific group of people (family or neighbors) or location (the workplace or school). Here are a few ideas:

1. Announce that the Bible studies will be weekly and have a specific duration (*e.g.,* eight weeks).
2. Pick a date/time one month in advance to announce to potential attendees.
3. Who to invite: one solid Christian couple and ten to fifteen unsaved souls or weak Christians.
4. Ten to fourteen days prior to the first meeting, mail flyers about the study to those you have contacted.
5. Personally call potential attendees two to three days in advance.
6. Ideal study size is about seven to ten (perhaps fewer if just unsaved people attend).
7. Not everyone who says "we'll come" will come.
8. Be prepared for many ups and downs (remember that God is molding you, too).

There are two points to make here. I make no apologies for politely "pressuring" people to attend the first study. Most folks will feel ashamed in not coming to at least the first study if over the last month you have contacted them four or five times (either verbally, by e-mail or snail mail). The objective is to get them to the first study. Again, there is something contagious about excitement! If folks see your excitement about the study, they will normally come.

Secondly, often a person will tell me that he or she is a Christian, although I have serious doubts about their salvation. It is not my function to tell people whether they are saved or not. That is the Holy Spirit's work according to Romans 8:14-17. Neither do I know or search the hearts of men; the Lord does that, according to 1 Samuel 16:7 and Revelation 2:23. The best approach is to neither acknowledge nor deny their claims to be Christians until you have good evidence to do so by their spiritual behavior. As the

Lord said, *"Either make the tree good, and his fruit good; or else make the tree corrupt, and his fruit corrupt: for the tree is known by his fruit"* (Mt. 12:33). The more that these individuals are in the Word of God, the more time God has to personally talk with them. Try to keep them coming by affirming their attendance, good answers, and participation in the discussion, but don't confirm them as saved by calling them "brother" or "sister." In the end, if the Lord doesn't show them that they need salvation, nothing you say or do will matter.

So as not to cause unnecessary division in an evangelistic study, it is best not to refer to other Christians as brother or sister either, as those who do not receive this title will understand that you consider them different, possibly not a Christian.

The Lord has allowed me to start numerous Bible studies throughout various times of the year. I have found the most opportune times to be in early February and early September. Remember, you have to start planning a month in advance of these start dates. Practically, people have recovered from holiday stress by mid-January, and on the sports scene, football is nearly done and baseball, soccer, and softball are three months away. In the fall, school has started, family routines are solidifying again, and you have time to start the study before Thanksgiving arrives.

Regardless of what type of outreach study you are considering, the following words of Ada Lum from his book, *How to Begin an Evangelistic Bible Study,* will help you maintain the right attitude in your mind.

The Evangelistic Bible Study (EBS) is demanding because it requires our best all-around efforts as "beggars." (D. T. Niles has defined a Christian witness as "one beggar telling another beggar where to find food.") It requires that we regard the inquiring non-believer as a whole person, not merely as a "soul." He or she is a person with intelligence, feelings, and integrity of individual will. The EBS requires that we "give ourselves away" as fellow human beings, just as Paul did to the Thessalonians (1 Thess. 2:8).

The EBS is a contrast and complement to other evangelistic methods. Much of our evangelism is extensive—large lecture meetings, special missions, musical programs, etc. Or it is communicating the gospel directly or indirectly during brief encounters with strangers, as in sharing our faith with a seat companion on the train, giving out tracts, knocking on doors and other short-lived contacts.

But most of us normally live in a settled community. Here we have the responsibility of intense evangelism, that is, concentrating on one or two or three seekers in a sustained way. Here nothing is more effective than the personal evangelistic Bible study fellowship. Here we can invite our friends who show confusion, vagueness or a fragmented knowledge of the gospel. Here none of us will feel rushed or pressured but can calmly examine the facts about Jesus Christ.[1]

7

The Hardest Study— The First One

The first study is the hardest one. Besides having a room full of strangers, people come late, some not at all, and most are naturally a bit nervous. This is where the home environment and a good sense of humor will really be a plus. At the first study, discuss openly what will be studied. It is best if the leader determines the study material or book of the Bible to be used for the initial series, then allows the group to decide where to go from there with helpful guidance from the teacher. Most questions in the first study will be "open" type questions to the group. Asking direct questions of individuals, before you understand how they feel about the study or talking in front of strangers can frighten the shy or hesitant from coming again. Through general questioning, identify what the group wants to get out of this Bible study experience.

Ascertaining the needs of individuals in the group is accomplished by careful observation during the study. The leader should be attentive and then do a little "fishing" with non-threatening questions to fill in the missing information. You may ask questions like, "What kind of family environment did you grow up in?" If someone claims to be a Christian, ask "How did you become a Christian?" or "What area of your spiritual life needs the most attention?" The answers to these questions will give you insights about whether the person truly understands the gospel, if there is a history of religious baggage, or if there is a need for further instruction in a particular area of doctrine (like water baptism). Most importantly, you must "learn" the person to know how to minister to them! Don't jump on wrong answers. You are not engaged in correcting unscriptural beliefs at this time, but in understanding individual needs.

Agree to a general goal for the study, then tactfully obtain attendee commitment to accomplish this goal in an agreed-to amount of time. My experience has shown that getting some level of commitment from attendees during the first session will yield a higher attendee-retention rate through the study. This may vary from person to person. Some people will be willing to commit for the entire study series whereas others will agree just for the next time.

A man named "Dick" came the first night of a recent outreach study. While in the introduction stage of the study, he bluntly said, "I don't know if I'll be back and please don't be offended if I just get up and leave during this study." My response was, "We are very glad you came tonight, Dick, and since the Bible is our only authority in this study, if you hear something that alarms you enough to leave, please tell me about it because I am accountable to God to stay true to His Word." Dick didn't leave that night and, in fact, came back for several more studies.

Roberta Hestenes first popularized the concept of group commitment (at least in recent years). Her "covenant" style approach for small group meetings became the model for many to follow. Lyman Coleman explains,

Every group needs to decide on a covenant: What is our purpose?

Also, decide how long you are going to meet. Then, as a group, evaluate your progress before renewing your covenant for a longer period.[1]

The "covenant" supplies the common discipline needed to make the group stick together and be focused. Although the author is not advocating a written agreement or a "covenant" approach to the study, there is something to be said for obtaining some level of commitment from the attendees. Be honest with them about how much time it will take each week to adequately prepare for the study.

Besides discussing what will be studied, deriving personal goals for the study and obtaining some level of commitment to continue in the study, allow plenty of time for tangents that first meeting. Often people have questions that they have wanted to ask all their lives. If they get satisfactory answers, they will be back the next week with more questions. Many who come to the study will know nothing about the Bible. For some, it is a mysterious book. For others, it is an untouchable book. Make the Bible a reachable book. Generally, a ten-minute overview of the Bible will help make the Bible more accessible.

Describe the four main sections of the Old Testament:
- LAW—reveals God's holiness in commandments
- HISTORY—the "story line" of the OT
- POETRY—praise and practical wisdom
- PROPHECY

In the New Testament:
- THE GOSPELS—reveal God's holiness in Christ
- HISTORY—ACTS, the story of the early Church
- EPISTLES—letters of practical truth and wisdom
- PROPHECY—REVELATION, God's last word to man

Note the symmetry of construction between testaments. This might be a great time to give some hints for finding books in the Bible. For examples, the Book of Psalms is in the middle of the Bible. If you half the Bible again toward the back, you will come to Matthew, the first book in the New Testament. The books starting with the letter "Z" in the Bible are towards the end of the Old Testament. The books starting with the letter "T" in the New Testament are together and in alphabetical order. The crucifixion chapters in the four Gospel accounts are spaced in differences of "4": Mark 15, John 19, Luke 23 and Matthew 27.

Be prepared to give some historical information on the Bible and how various translations and versions developed. This subject will often surface during the first few studies, possibly the first study. Much more resource material is given to the reader on this subject in an Appendix (p. 123).

Generally, after a few tangents and questions, I will have the group turn to the book of Genesis and read portions from chapters 2, 3 and 4. From these texts, the questioning, discussion and discovery begins. The fall of man is seen, sin is defined, and God's solution in "types" is unveiled from the opening pages of the Bible (redemption through Christ—Gen. 3:15; 3:21; 4:4-5).

The first study is so important in securing people to come again. How do you create a home-study environment, which puts people at ease during the first study? Howard Hendricks gives the following helpful tips.[2]

    a. Arrange your living room (or den or whatever room the class will meet in) to provide a friendly, informal atmosphere.

    b. Aim at making everyone feel at ease.

    c. Avoid church expressions.

    d. Be natural and casual in your attitude and actions.

    e. Have newcomers sign a guest book.

    f. Learn the people's names. Be sure to introduce newcomers to the group.

g. Have extra Bibles on hand (of a readable translation—I suggest NKJV or NAS).

h. After most attendees have gone, some will want to stay to ask questions of the teacher. Be prepared to let them stay.

I have two follow-up comments to Mr. Hendrick's list. First, if you are nervous, you will make the attendees nervous. Relax, the Creator of the universe is on your side. Second, you run the risk of instantly turning people off if you use religious phrases, "buzz words" or make references to Christian labels (Baptist, Catholic, etc.).

One man told me, after he was saved through a one-on-one Bible study, that if I had mentioned being "born again" or "needing salvation" to him, he would have promptly walked out. He said, "I didn't want anything to do with those born again Christians." Now that he is one of those "born again" types, he is seeing things differently, but he didn't at first. Be careful. Let the Scripture speak for itself.

If the "denomination label" irritation surfaces, it can cause division in the group before you even get started. So, quickly nip it in the bud. The leader should turn the conversation from religion back to the Saviour. Perhaps tell the group, "I want you to understand something about me. I am neither a Roman Catholic nor a Protestant (I am not protesting against anything). The Bible is the sole authority in my life, Jesus Christ is the Lord of my life, and all I want to do is please Him. The only way I can know what my life is about, know God, and know His will for me is by studying His Word. I hope you came tonight for the same reason."

Generally, a statement like this, which declares you are pro-God and not out to please a church, brings a hush of neutrality over the group and allows the study to continue in peace.

The climate you create in the first study is so important. Everything about the study should say, "We love you and we are so glad you came!" First impressions are important: think about details like having a pot of hot coffee or tea, perhaps fresh flowers for a women's study. A warm greeting and learning names quickly will go far in starting things out on the right foot. Sometimes sharing a bizarre news clipping, a funny story, a cartoon or a poem can break the ice to get things off and running.

8

Bibles, Study Aids and Materials

BIBLES

What Bible translation should be used for a Bible study? There are differing opinions, but certainly a modern version will improve group readability and understanding of the text. Whether the study is a discipleship study or an evangelical outreach study, I encourage folks to stick with a literal translation. What is a literal translation? It is a specific kind of translation that expresses, as much as possible, the exact meaning of the original language, word-for-word.

There are four versions I try to steer attendees to in Bible studies. Three are literal translations (KJV, NKJV, and NASV); the fourth (and my last choice of the four) is a readable but less "formal" (word-for-word) translation of the Bible, the NIV. Attendees will find it easier to use language study tools later in investigating word meanings if they use a literal translation.

Paraphrased versions of the Bible are restatements of

passages in an attempt to keep the original sense while expressing the meaning in a clear and readable fashion. However, the feature of free expression is often at the expense of language detail and accuracy. The Living Bible, for example, is a popular paraphrase of the Bible, and because of its relaxed readability, often shows up at outreach studies. Sometimes just explaining to people that a father (Ken Taylor) created this retelling for his children so they would be able to understand the Bible will help to explain paraphrases. As much as possible, try to discourage the use of paraphrases of the Bible in the studies, but don't make an issue of it if someone keeps bringing one along.

For discipleship studies, more than one translation is often a plus; but for outreach studies, I encourage people to bring their own Bible if they have one, but to also take one of the paperback Bibles that I have available at the study. Reading from one version of the Bible instead of several minimizes confusion. Providing the attendees with reliable paperback versions of the Bible also removes the threat of a poor or flawed translation from corrupting the Scripture reading, such as the New World Translation. The other practical benefit of using a common paperback version is the ease of finding books in the Bible by calling out page numbers. This is a practice that, after a few studies, will naturally die out, as attendees become more familiar with the layout of the Bible.

Bible translations are often a topic of discussion in an outreach study. Usually this is because, just hours earlier, someone blew the dust off of their coffee table Bible or found a long-lost version on a bookshelf in the basement and brought it to the study. They want to know about the version they have. Generally, a ten-minute overview of Bible translations and history is profitable to the group. I have included some relevant information on this subject in an Appendix (p. 123) to aid the leader in this discussion.

The Bible overview given by the study leader need not (should not) include all of the information in this appendix; just hit the high points. That information has been provided to the teacher for a quick reference in the event you're questioned or challenged about the validity of the Bible.

Be sensitive to an individual's religious orientation. For example, a woman might bring her family Catholic Bible to the study. Don't discourage her from bringing it (it contains the truth also) but be sure to place a paperback Bible in her hands as well. Tell her she can read both texts and determine which is easier to read.

Oftentimes a question arises about the Apocrypha in the first study or two. I simply say that most of the Apocryphal books (fifteen in all) provide an historical link between the New and Old Testaments (a four-hundred-year silence by God). Without the Apocrypha we would be missing some elements of Jewish history, for example, personal Jewish accounts of the Syrian campaign led by Antiochus Epiphanes in 168 BC against Jerusalem. We learn of Jewish suffering at this time and how the Jews rallied behind Judas Maccabaeus to drive the Syrians out.

In general, the Apocrypha consists of Jewish literature, poetry and history and is not relevant to Christian doctrine. Why were they not recognized as canonical? Edward J. Young writes in his book, *Revelation and the Bible:*

> The answer must be that these books were not regarded as divinely inspired. This statement, however, involves certain questions. How can one tell that a book is inspired? Is it always possible to discover a book's quality of inspiration?…There are no marks in these [apocryphal] books which would attest a divine origin. As William Henry

Green (in his book *General Introduction of the Old Testament, The Canon*) has pointed out, both Judith and Tobit contain historical, chronological and geographical errors. The books justify falsehood and deception and make salvation to depend upon works of merit. Almsgiving, for example, is said to deliver from death (Tobit 12:9; 4:10; 14:10-11).

Judith lives a life of falsehood and deception in which she is represented as assisted by God (9:10, 13). Ecclesiasticus and the Wisdom of Solomon inculcate a morality based upon expediency. Wisdom teaches the creation of the world out of pre-existent matter (11:17). Ecclesiasticus teaches that the giving of alms makes atonement for sin (3:30). In Baruch it is said that God hears the prayers of the dead (3:4), and in 1 Maccabees there are historical and geographical errors. This is not to deny many fine and commendable things in the Apocrypha, but the books nonetheless show themselves at points to be at variance with divinely revealed truth. They were consequently never adopted by the Jews as canonical.[1]

In some cases, the authors of the Apocryphal books themselves state that their writings are not divinely inspired (1 Maccabees 9:27 and 14:41) and even apologize for the way that the books are written (2 Maccabees 15:38). Certainly, if the book was divinely inspired, no apologies are needed for its textual content. It might be good to inform the attendee that even the Roman Catholic Church did not officially recognize the Apocryhpha as canonical until the Counter Reformation Period (via the Council of Trent, held between 1545 and 1563 AD).[2]

Why is this information helpful? Because the Catholic doctrine of "purgatory" comes from a story in 2 Maccabees 12:40-42. This doctrine did not become an official Catholic dogma until 1439 at the Council of Florence, although it was first introduced 850 years earlier by Pope Gregory the Great in 593.[3] If you can prove to your attendee that the writer was not inspired by God in writing 2 Maccabees, the doctrine of purgatory then clearly becomes a tradition of the church and not a doctrine of the Bible.

One last thought concerning Bible translations: The leader would be wise to plan the scriptural course for the study ahead of time in order to avoid (at least at first) difficulties between Majority vs. Critical based translations. For example, if someone in the group was reading Matthew 18:11, Acts 8:37 or 1 John 5:7 from a NASV or NIV, they might comment on a manuscript note in their Bible. Or someone with a NKJV might say, "Hey, you skipped some words." These rare anomalies don't change Bible doctrine, but can cause some to believe the Bible is not textually reliable. Having paperback Bibles available of a single literal translation will reduce the probability of this situation occurring. Perhaps choose a translation that your local church prefers or gravitates to. In this way, if participants comes to Christ, they will have no difficulty following along in their Bibles once church attendance begins.

COMMENTARIES, CONCORDANCES AND STUDY BIBLES

If after three or four meetings it seems like the attendees are getting comfortable finding passages and reading their Bibles, introduce the group to some other study helps. A good commentary and concordance will greatly help students through the week to be able to dig a little deeper with the assistance of a theologian in their back pocket. However, a fallacy some will fall into—if not adequately warned—is to ascribe inspiration to the commentary. Ensure that the Bible remains at the center of the group's attention, and study tools are secondary. These tools are helpful, but of a human origin and therefore not perfect.

It is a good practice to have some reliable commentaries

on hand and to allow the attendees to experience their help through the week. Simply explain that they can try one out and, if they like it, state the cost of purchase. If they don't don't like it, they can just bring it back. Through the years of teaching Bible studies, I have had perhaps three or four attendees return a commentary. If people are poor, ask them to pay you for a portion of the commentary. Generally, it will mean more to them if they pay you something for it instead of you giving it to them.

There are many good commentaries, but my favorite full Bible commentary to put in the hands of attendees (for an outreach or discipleship study) is the *Believer's Bible Commentary* by William MacDonald (Thomas Nelson). This commentary is easy to read, devotional, sound in doctrine, and endorsed by many solid Christians. Warren Wiersbe writes that this commentary is "for the student who is serious about seeing Christ in the Word."

If you use a study Bible, perhaps introduce the attendees to it through a few practical activities. You could use a chain reference, read some commentary notes aloud, or demonstrate the concordances.

We live in an age when there is a devotional Bible for everyone: singles, youth, women, men, the aged, etc. My personal favorite study Bibles are the New Scofield and the Ryrie Study Bibles. There are other good ones available; offer to order one for attendees if they wish.

After several more weeks, you might introduce the group to other tools: Bible software, language dictionaries, interlinear Bibles, other commentaries, etc. Be careful not to overwhelm people or lead them to think they need to have a small fortune in study tools to understand the Bible.

Of course if and when they become Christians, the best Teacher of the Bible is the Holy Spirit Himself (Jn. 16:13).

STUDY MATERIALS

The study material selected must be at the level of group comprehension. For an evangelical outreach study, I prefer to begin with the book of Romans or John or with one of two study workbooks: *Survey in Basic Christianity* (SBC) or *Basic Christian Training* (BCT) by O. Jean Gibson (Walterick).

SBC covers the fundamentals: man's depravity, his fallen situation and God's solution. BCT covers the basics of the Christian faith, but the first few lessons are largely gospel. Sometimes people come to the BCT study believing they are Christians, but in a few weeks, learn they are not and become Christians through gospel exposure. There is nothing like being in God's Word to expose the truth about one's soul. I recall one man who professed to be a Christian, but after a few studies discovered he was not. He excitedly declared what he had found out, "I knew stories about Jesus, I knew who He was (God's Son), but I didn't know Him personally. I didn't understand that He loved me personally and died my death on the cross. Now I know Jesus is the Saviour of my soul."

Questions for book studies in the Bible should be prepared a week in advance to allow participants to discover truth through the week. We will talk more about developing questions in a later chapter. But perhaps ten to twelve questions, which challenge but don't choke, are appropriate. Students should leave each study with a deeper realization of God and what their response should be in pleasing Him.

No matter what questions or study material is used, ensure that answering written questions doesn't become the ruler for completing the study. There is a tendency to think that, when all the written questions given the week before are covered, the study is over. However, the purpose of the written questions is to give accountability for the attendees to study through the week and to be wisely prepared for discussion. There will be much more to derive from the text. A good leader will adequately cover the text and use the study questions as a tool to initiate discussion in bringing further discovery to the group.

9

Teaching a Bible Study

How does one teach a Bible study and apply the Scriptures in a lasting way? Michael Wiebe suggests that you challenge those attending the study to ask three basic questions about the passage of Scripture being studied:

- What does it say? (observation; gathering facts—who, where, when, what);
- What does it mean? (interpreting the facts);
- What does it mean to me? (applying the interpretation to our own life).[1]

The Navigator summarizes these three steps as discover, understanding, and application.[2]

Discover. A discover question should be short, relevant, and easily understood. Did anyone in the group find out anything about...? Did someone learn something new about the culture of the day in this Scripture passage?

Understanding. Remove any hard words that may be blocking understanding by defining them from a concordance and related scriptures. Relate other passages on the context of the passage to give the big picture. Perhaps some questions which contrast or compare aspects of this section or topic with other parallel passages. Is there a meaning or a prophecy beyond the visible teaching to the audience at hand, or perhaps a type or shadow of the Lord Jesus to be found? Understanding what the passage "says" requires understanding the scriptural context and the facts of the passage—who is being addressed and why.

Application. How do I get members of the study to internalize the lesson and make it personal? Ask questions or give illustrations that will help them remember the lesson. Give them ways of practicing this lesson in day-to-day life and perhaps have some weekly follow-up questions to maintain accountability.

Marilyn Kunz in *Christianity Today* offers the following helpful hints in teaching a Bible study through attendee involvement and discovery.

A Bible study that is leader-centered tends to make the leader and not the Scripture the authority for the group. To enable a non-expert to participate in effective discussion leadership, it is necessary to use a study guide that stimulates every participant to make discoveries in the Bible text, but at the same time keeps the group on the main track. Care should be taken in selecting a study guide to avoid curriculum where the answers follow the questions; that makes the curriculum writer rather than the Scripture the authority.

It is true, of course, that someone who directs the discussion regularly derives the greatest benefit from the study. It is hard for such a leader to recognize that what he enjoys doing does not necessarily best help the other group members to learn. Everyone learns more when allowed to be responsible and involved. I recall a television program about educational excellence that showed a large sign one teacher hung in the back of her classroom:

I hear—I forget; I see—I remember; I do—I understand

All people learn more when they participate fully in their own education.[3]

Flexibility is important in a study group because it is easy to get stuck in a routine. As people come to Christ and grow in Him, they will develop distinctly different needs and aptitudes than when they first began meeting with you. Study dynamics must change as the needs of the people change. It could be that your evangelical study becomes a discipleship study. Great! Maybe you could consider starting another outreach study for unsaved contacts while reserving the first study for teaching young Christians. The study must meet the needs of those in the groups.

If the study seems to be getting stale, pray about changing the format and doing something a bit different. Perhaps gather prayer requests at the end of a study and have a time of prayer or share a few short "praise reports" from the previous week at the start of a study. Even moving the group to a different room of the house can help (perhaps move from the living room to the kitchen for a few weeks).

The study leader does not control the study; that is the Holy Spirit's job. The study leader simply leads the group by promoting discussion, personal evaluation, and growth through God's Word, the source of counsel for these matters. In discipleship studies, the leader will learn to spot non-biblical behavioral bents and apply the Scripture in an effort to exhort and gently reprove. The teacher should then seek to show the replacement scriptural grace (see Eph. 4:17-32) and then lend accountability to help the struggling believer. This is the essence of biblical counseling.

Don't commit the mistake with the group that many husbands make when they first come home from work and their wives begin to vent their frustrations. Fight the urge to be a problem solver. Men especially like to go for the quick fix and give advice to solve someone else's problems. It is important for hurting souls to express the ill that is causing them emotional pain and hindering spiritual growth. Listen intently. Don't interrupt. Ask a few questions to obtain the big picture. Repeat back to them portions of what they have said to let them know you are listening and care. Once you have the facts, then turn to Scripture and prayer to start the healing process.

It may be that their hurts stem from consequences of poor decisions or sins in the past. Help them see from Scripture the error of their ways and their need for repentance. Aid them to understand the biblical pattern of moving forward in God's will. It may be that a friend or family member has abused someone in your Bible study (very common, especially with women). Help them to see forgiveness is divine and pleases God. Forgiveness is Godlike. Help them to give the gift of forgiveness to the offending party as a means of sharing Christ with them and achieving personal release. Unforgiveness in the heart will be a bitter experience and will stifle fellowship with God.

Lyman Coleman accounts the following story to illustrate this point:

A few years ago I was in a group with Jim. He was a great guy and a real joker. But I had the feeling that he was covering up something painful in his past. We were studying the Lord's Prayer when Jim commented, "I could never refer to God as 'Father'—not with the father I had." I asked, "Jim, would you like to tell us about your father?"

After a long pause he said, "My father worked on the railroad. He was away from home a lot. When he came home, he was often drunk and violent. He abused my mother, and if I said anything, he would grab me and throw me out of the house."

There was another awkward silence as we struggled with our own feelings. Finally, Betty reached over, took his hand and said softly, "Jim, thank you for sharing that." Betty said the only thing that could have been said at that moment. She affirmed Jim. She thanked him. She did not try to "cure" him.[4]

Sometimes we try to "fix" people when they express a problem, and we end up driving the hurting person out of the group. We should care, but rely on God's assistance to cure. It usually takes time. The leader needs to convey and nurture a caring atmosphere in the group that tells everyone they are important, but at the same time does not compromise divine directives or personal holiness.

How does the leader know if the study is going well? Perhaps this quick leader's evaluation checklist from the Navigators will be helpful.

- Did everyone expected come to the meeting?
- Did everyone present take part in the discussion?
- Was it a lecture, conversation, or true discussion?
- Did anyone become the group leader?
- Did the discussion lead to further understanding of the truths they had discovered in their personal study time?
- Did you guide the discussion with questions?
- Did you summarize adequately?
- Did you keep to the subject?
- Was there enough time for sharing written applications?
- Were the applications practical and possible?
- Did you end on time?
- Were there any positive results from the previous written applications?[5]

10

Bible Studies in the Workplace

Although the techniques used in leading a home Bible study or a workplace study don't vary much, the dynamics do. In your home, you are the sole authority that addresses issues or problems that arise. However, in the workplace, there are authorities and corporate policies that must be considered before you initiate a Bible study. For example, if there are known written policies which limit spiritual meetings on company premises, then you would be wrong to begin a Bible study without investigating the policy and seeking permission. Perhaps a Bible study would be allowed if not conducted during normal work hours. In any case, Paul clearly teaches in Romans 13:1-2 that we are to be subject to the authorities that are over us because all authority is placed by God.

Practically speaking, the reader will find very few (if any) company policies which limit an employee's use of non-work time. Such a policy would become a legal night-mare to enforce, as many employees engage in non-work related personal activities on company premises during work breaks and the lunch hour. These include football pools, playing cards, reading books, playing video games and having internet chat sessions. Would it be appropriate for a company to permit employees to use a conference room to play poker during lunch, but not allow them to discuss their faith? Beside all this, it is easier to ask for forgiveness than to ask for permission! The author has had no past difficulties holding Bible studies on company premises.

Here are a few guidelines to consider in avoiding company problems with workplace studies. Remember, non-believers will be watching, and some will be seeking some issue to bring accusation. The best way to avoid this is to be blameless in every aspect of the study (like Daniel was before his enemies, Dan. 6:4-5).

Be blameless in your meeting time. If you have an hour for lunch, don't take an hour and ten minutes. That would be stealing from the company. If you meet before the normal workday begins, be sure to end on time. It may seem to some that you are meeting longer than the allotted time because you start a lunch break study slightly early. Try to adhere to the normal break schedules generally followed by most employees even if you have "flex time." Blameless is a step beyond not doing anything wrong—it is conduct that will not even bring an accusation of wrong doing.

A woman named Mrs. Reed comments on how the Bible study in her workplace manages time to remain blameless. "We meet for forty-five minutes. We only get a half-hour for lunch, but some of us combine our lunchtime with coffee break. Others come late or leave a little early. The store lets us do it."[1]

Pick a quiet and private place for your study. The location of the study should not interfere with other employees who are working, and other employees who are working should not distract from the study. A conference room works better than an office of an attendee because the telephone will still ring and people will stop by to visit. Some might see this hindrance to business coordination as impeding company productivity.

If possible, reserve a conference room for the study. Most conference rooms will have schedules that you can reserve weekly. Since few meetings continue through the lunch hour, you will likely get good availability. Try to meet in the same place each week to limit confusion among attendees. Also, it is important to be flexible. If you arrive at the conference room and a meeting is in progress, simply ask the folks if they are close to wrapping up. If not, just have the study group meet in another conference room. This means that the study leader should have a back-up plan. Again, you are blameless. You are not hindering company business because of a Bible study.

If management is involved with the study, you further diminish the likelihood of possible company problems. If you have a Christian manager or two in your study, it will generally ease any concerns of other managers that there is a covert religious organization planning a corporate takeover!

One advantage that the workplace has over the home is that it is more conducive to multiple weekly Bible studies. For example, you may have a small outreach evangelical study on Thursday and a discipleship study on Tuesday. As people are saved from the outreach studies, you move them into the discipleship study. The discipleship study becomes an ongoing place of spiritual discovery and provides an opportunity to test and develop a teaching gift.

Are you ready for a workplace Bible study? If not, perhaps this true story by Stuart McAllister will encourage you to step out in faith.

When I accepted a job transfer to Cleveland in 1978, I hoped to find a weekly lunchtime Bible study like the one I had attended during my last position in Columbus, but my search for a downtown Bible study was fruitless.

One September day at noon, I watched people heading for lunch in the streets below my office window. They want food, I thought, but most of them don't know the Bread of Life. At that moment, I realized God wanted me to start a workplace Bible study, not find one. The idea frightened me: I had never taught adults before.

After weeks of prayer, I called the company's service bureau to reserve a meeting room. "For what date, sir?" the attendant asked pleasantly.

"Wednesday, January 3, next year," I said. "And every Wednesday after that, from noon to one."

"Sir," she said, puzzled by the unusual time, "is this a business meeting?"

"Not exactly. I'd like to start an employee Bible study."

"Oh, I see."

"Oh course," I interjected, "I want to be very flexible about it. We'll cancel the study anytime the room is needed for business. On a moment's notice, really."

"I understand," she said coolly. "Just a moment, please, while I check with my supervisor." I fired up my best on-hold prayer. She returned with a surprising question: "How many people will be attending the meeting each week?"

"I'm not sure," I confessed. "Not too many at first, until word gets around." Go for broke, I told myself. "Can we get a room that will allow for growth through the year? Say up to twenty-five people?"

"All right. We can do that, but if the room is needed for official business…"

"Yes, ma'am," I said. "You'll have our full cooperation on that."

Then came God's next surprise. "If you can get Graphic Arts to prepare some posters," she offered, "we'll distribute them to all employee bulletin boards in the complex." I did, and the posters were hung in early December, one month before our first meeting. On the advice of a pastor, I decided to teach the Gospel of John. It's ideal for an evangelistic Bible study, he said, because it reveals Jesus as God and the Saviour of all who believe.

On the day of the first study, I went to the meeting room a few minutes early to pray and make final preparations. I was shocked to find the room half-filled. By noon, all twenty-five seats were occupied. [2]

Stuart goes on to tell of the fruitfulness of this study in reaching souls for Christ. For some studies, a bigger meeting room was necessary. Numerous other studies "hived off" the original study. After thirteen years, twelve books of the Bible had been thoroughly covered. Stuart continued teaching this lunch time study until he retired from the company.

Could God repeat this miracle at your place of work? He can if you will trust and rely on Him.

11

Stimulating Teens to Grow

Teens can be one of the most challenging age groups to stimulate to spiritual maturity. The teen culture, which has dominated secular advertising, amusements, and family pastimes for nearly two decades, has made teaching teens more difficult. Video games, computer entertainment of all sorts, sport activities galore, and public education's shift from moral absolutes and reasoning skills have all contributed to "an over-entertained and under-challenged" generation of young people. How do you teach young people in our generation? With great creativity and patience.

Here are a few suggestions to get your youth studies progressing heavenward. First of all—forget entertainment! That which is secular, ungodly, that which stirs the flesh in lieu of the spirit will never promote spiritual growth.

> *Now we have received, not the spirit of the world, but the Spirit who is of God; that we might know the things that are freely given to us of God. Which things also we speak, not in the words which man's wisdom teacheth, but which the Holy Spirit teacheth; comparing spiritual things with spiritual"* (1 Cor. 2:12-13).

Although the author abhors the term, because it promotes segregation within the assembly, many "youth groups" today are typically entertainment-oriented instead of ministry- and study-focused. It is through spiritual growth and spiritual service that young people receive abiding joy and not a cheap high from some momentary stimulation of the flesh. Laser tag, paint ball, mazes, and the like may have their place, but if young people desire to do these types of activities, they should schedule the outings on their own so that the Lord's money and His servants' time are not squandered meaninglessly. Parents should oversee these outings—the church need not "teen sit."

In general, teaching young people today is an emotional roller coaster ride—so fasten your safety belt of truth and hold on to sound, Spirit-led principles. You will find teaching youth whose parents have good and enforced boundaries at home much easier than those whose parents have few boundaries, who allow their children to dabble in the world. It has been the author's experience that one of the main channels of worldliness into the church is through young people whose parents have not properly trained their children in holy living. These students will be more difficult to teach and motivate spiritually. But there is also more at stake. It will be through them that secular ideologies seep into the local church. So for the good of the assembly and for these struggling teens, significant expenditure of personal time and energy must be made. Teen ministry is not a once-a-month or even a weekend effort. It requires constant attention, effort, compassion—and a thick skin!

The power of prayer will be the transforming factor of any successful teen study, but here are three tangible areas of study dynamics that the leader should concentrate on: good music, involvement, and frequent format changes during your time together.

Music is very important to most young people today. However, the guidelines Paul lays down for music would exclude a good portion of the "contemporary Christian music" which one might hear on the radio today.

Speaking to yourselves in psalms and hymns and spiritual songs, singing,and making melody in your heart to the Lord (Eph. 5:19).

Let the word of Christ dwell in you richly, in all wisdom; teaching and admonishing one another, in psalms and hymns, and spiritual songs, singing with grace in your hearts to the Lord (Col. 3:16).

What the believer sings should be based on the Word of God directly, or derived from the wisdom the Word gives.

A great way to start youth studies is to have one of the young people play a guitar and then have others choose solid praise songs to sing. Perhaps devote fifteen minutes to this before the study begins. If there is a song that doesn't make much sense or one that resembles a pagan chant (sometimes called a "seven-eleven" song—sing seven words eleven times) perhaps allow the group to analyze the song and make a group decision whether it should be sung in the future. By singing without instruments or simply with a guitar or piano, you avoid stimulating the flesh by heavy back-beats which are prevalent in much of the secular music today. These stir the flesh. It is the author's opinion that young people should leave their own music tapes and CDs at home and not bring them to assembly meetings, youth meetings or on ministry outings unless the individual in charge has given approval ahead of time. This may seem like a hard-line assault on personal rights, but this better protects the liberty of others, and ensures that a weaker brother or sister will not be stumbled (1 Cor. 8:9) or the gospel will not be hindered (1 Cor. 9:12).

Involvement builds commitment. Your study format

should be such that everyone takes part. Actually, teen meetings are a great way to teach young people how to plan meals or refreshments for large groups. Perhaps, on a rotation basis, put different young people in charge of coordinating and delegating responsibilities for preparing a meal before a teen study, or a time of refreshment during the study. Have one person in charge of leading music, another to open in prayer and another to close in prayer. Engage those who are quiet by direct questions. Have everyone read Scripture (have each person read one verse and circulate around the room).

Teens seem to do better focusing on spiritual studies if the format and topics of the study are a bit dynamic. Allow for tangents and questions during studies. Take a break in the middle of your study for refreshments and then gather again for edification via a different study format. Here are some studies formats to consider in your next teen study.

DEBATES

About one to two weeks ahead of the next teen study, hand out a sheet with debate assignments. This is an enjoyable way to study a particular subject in Scripture. The accountability to prepare for the debate is that each teen does not what to be outdone by his opponent. Try to match students according to their knowledge of Scripture and astuteness in study, and give the harder debate topics to the more mature young people, challenging the older ones in the Lord with tougher subjects. However, be sure to rotate who debates with whom so no lasting rivalries develop.

Each student gets three minutes to present his or her position and then two minutes to counter the other's position. Encourage all students to have a "Teen Study" folder in which they can file study and debate notes from each meeting. They should bring this file to every study—it will provide a central archive of information that they can look back on for years to come. After each debate is completed, spend about fifteen minutes in conclusion. Encourage good points made, complete what is incomplete, and gently correct what is in error (humor may be used to smooth and lighten the correction process, but not at the expense of the debater). Review other passages of scripture to further solidify the proper biblical position. Here are a few of the debates the teens in our local assembly have done :

The Holy Spirit is not a person, but a force, an influence.
First position: False—the Holy Spirit is a person (don't approach from divinity argument)
Second position: True—the Holy Spirit is an influence

The Holy Spirit is God.
First position: True
Second position: False—the Holy Spirit is not God.

Jesus Christ is Michael the archangel in bodily form.
First position: False—Christ is the only Son of God
Second position: True

God is everything and therefore everything deserves our adoration (Pantheism).
First position: False—God manifests Himself in creation, but does not constitute creation.
Second position: True

The Bible is flawed so we need further revelation or new study books to address the errors and to properly interpret corrupt passages.
First position: False—God's Word has been preserved so

that we might know His will.
Second position: True

A human soul is not immortal. It either dies when man dies or is annihilated in judgment.
First position: False—a soul is immortal and will either enjoy the eternal presence of God or everlasting torment.
Second position: True

The millennium of Christ reign is spiritually occurring now. There is no literal 1000 year earthly reign of peace on earth by Christ.
First position: True
Second position: False: We are not living in the period known as the millennium; it is still future.

There is no difference between Israel and the Church in God's eyes; they are all God's people and will enjoy the same status and position in heaven.
First position: True
Second position: False

SPEECHES

Public speaking is a phobia for many, so why not help young people overcome their fears early in life? A four-minute presentation will help students learn how to outline and organize subjects in a meaningful format to convey information. Even shy students don't seem to have much difficulty in sharing a speech with others of their own age who are being challenged to do the same. Misery loves company, but overcoming together promotes further cama-raderie! As with the debate format, take time after each speech to go over what has been said and what needs to be yet stated. This same format can be used for a book report or to do a biography on a "Hero of the Faith" or an obscure Bible character.

One teen study was devoted to the study of spiritual beings. The following were speech assignments for this study:

Identify and explain the biblical names of good angels
What are "foul spirits" and their work?
Who is Satan and his work?
What are characteristics of holy angels?
What are the ministries of holy angels?
What are demons and their work?
What are cherubim and their work?
What are "familiar spirits" and their work?
What are seraphim? Could they be the four living creatures?

Teen Chats

These are informal study sessions that usually have no intended subject. Young people gather together with their Bibles in a circle or around a table and the study goes where the Spirit leads. The hardest part of this kind of study is getting started, especially if some teens don't know each other. One method of starting is just to encourage open conversation about anything at the first and then base the study on what has been discussed—turn the discussion along a spiritual avenue. After a few minutes the questions usually start coming. Some young people have had questions eating at them for a long time, but they don't know how to phrase the question properly or they are afraid of looking stupid in front of adults. All questions and subjects should be addressed from Scripture, always asking the teens, "What does the Word say to you about this?"

MOVIE NIGHTS

By movie night we are not talking about watching movies for entertainment purposes, but for education and motivation. Many of the secularly produced G-rated animated movies can be used to demonstrate New Age propaganda. By showing segments of these movies, one can identify and discuss how the following pagan teachings are propagated: pantheism, animism, spirit guides, divination, necromancy, reincarnation, soul travel, levitation, etc. These teachings are often well disguised in humor, special effects, captivating music, or a love story. Good movies on future events, the life of Christ, Church history, heroes of the faith, etc., can be thought-provoking tools to inspire a deeper faith in Christ. Movies which dramatize the suffering of individuals who have converted to Christianity from other religions are helpful to teach discipleship and Lordship principles of the Christian faith. The movie should not become the main focus of the study—the purpose of the movie is to encourage further Bible study on the subject matter and to cause each individual to inventory their own dedication to the Saviour.

HOMEWORK

Study questions alone may seem a bit much, but a few questions combined with the above study formats normally aid preparation for the debate, speech, report, or review. Study questions should be available at least a week in advance, even though most will do them the night before the study. Be sure to leave the questions open-ended (phrases such as, "Identify principles for…" rather than "What eight principles are found in…?") Direct the student to a location in Scripture to find the answer. A little struggling is good, but don't overwhelm the student with difficult questions or forty-two scripture references to look up to answer your question. They may give up and not do any of the lesson.

BIBLE "TRIVIA" QUESTIONS

Bible "trivia" (nothing in the Bible is really trivia) or Bible clue games are a great way to have fun and learn more facts from Scripture. Boys against the girls seems to always stir up enough rivalry to create a legitimate educational, but happy atmosphere. However, if it is obvious that one gender is much more astute than the other, you will have to derive a more creative way of developing teams, such as by months of birth, alphabetical order, or some other way.

GUEST SPEAKERS

The main idea of inviting a guest speaker is allowing a group of teens to get as much variety as possible rather than to get stuck in the doldrums. This is especially successful if it is someone the young people respect.

COMBINING STUDY WITH MINISTRY

Discipleship of young people requires them to learn and appreciate the satisfaction that "self-giving" brings. Be sure to involve the young people in a balanced program of study and ministry. For evangelism, the following are suggested: short-term mission trips, door-to-door work, children's backyard Bible clubs, evangelistic skits and mimes, balloon ministry in the parks (hand children tracts with a balloon animal), and preparing outreach mailings or distribution of gospel literature in other ways.

For service, the following are possible: helping widows, the elderly, the sick or disabled by raking leaves, mowing yards, shoveling snow, baby-sitting, painting, etc. Support the local rescue mission by serving meals or taking part in a chapel service. Possibilities are endless. The combination of good works and the gospel is winsome to others and beneficial to teach our youth the joy of servanthood.

12

Questions, Questions, Questions

Unwritten questions during a small group study are one of the most powerful methods of stimulating, deepening, or changing the direction of a discussion. A group leader needs to think through both the written questions for the study assignment and verbal questions that will nurture a healthy dialogue during the actual group study. The written questions (for the following week's study) should be handed out at the conclusion of the study. These questions will help guide personal Bible study through the week on the part of the attendees and give accountability to do so. It is embarrassing to come to the study and not be prepared.

About eight to twelve written questions should be part of the study material each week. Questions specifically derived from Scripture and designed by the teacher for a particular group's need are the best. If you use re-packaged material, make sure to carefully evaluate the doctrine of the entire study before getting into the first lesson. The questions must be relevant to the passage of Scripture to be studied the following week. A good mix of textual, devotional and application questions is desirable. Good textual questions might be: "What is the context and theme of the passage?" or "What key verb reoccurs in this passage?" Devotional questions should cause the attendees to look at the Saviour (His character, His heart, His work). Application question should cause the attendees to look inside themselves: "What does this mean to me?"; "How should this affect my behavior?"; "What should my response be in obedience to Scripture?"

Verbalized questions can be categorized in different ways, but perhaps one of the simplest approaches is to evaluate to whom the question is directed. There are basically five ways to direct a question to a group.

a. Directed to oneself—rhetorical question
b. Directed to one member of the group—direct question
c. Directed to the one who asked the previous question—reverse question
d. Directed to anyone but the previous questioner—relay question
e. Directed to the group as a whole—general question

In general, rhetorical questions are for preachers and don't belong in small group studies. Rhetorical questions stifle group discussion because the leader has shifted from facilitation to overpowering the discussion.

Be careful with reverse questions, as the person asked may have nothing more to say. They may feel embarrassed, and say something under pressure that is wrong, which worsens the situation. The study leader will likely find that a combination of direct, general, and relay questions will stimulate group discussions forward, while still leaving enough steering control to keep the study on course.

Group and relay questions allow for good discussions, especially in smaller groups, but may tend to take too much time, especially if the study of Scripture has taken a back seat to stories and opinions. Direct questions serve four main purposes:

1. To engage the unengaging into the discussion.
2. To break the discussion away from someone in "lip lock."
3. To give needed accountability for an attendee to be in the Word throughout the week. (If they know that they are going to have to answer questions at the study, they will come to the study prepared.)
4. To engage someone who I know has a story, an experience or spiritual insight that benefits the discussion.

The purpose of the question must also be evaluated. The question may be designed to define facts, to clarify difficulties, to compare or contrast, or to develop the thought line. Sometimes a question can refocus the group back on the subject matter. Summary questions are good in getting the group to reiterate the conclusion just discovered. The Apostle Paul acknowledges the importance of reiterating learned truths (Gal. 3:1) so we don't forget.

Another facet of questioning is: "What answer does the question expect or suggest?" The following listing from the Navigators Log is helpful.

Type of Question: Leading
Examples: Of course you all agree, don't you?
Surely you don't think that, do you?
Answer: Yes/No
Value: None—it neither stimulates thought nor discussion.

Type of Question: Limiting
Example: What are the three great truths in this chapter?
Answer: What the group thinks you think
Value: None—it is clear to all you have an exact answer in mind. Instead of stimulating discussion, you have started a mind reading competition. It would be much better to leave out "the" and the number in your question. Then it becomes an open question.

Type of Question: Open
Examples: Who is this all about?
Where did this happen?
When was this?
Why was it?
What was the outcome?
How can anyone benefit?
Answer: People, places, times, reasons, results, etc.
Value: Much—it stimulates discovery, understanding, or application according to how you word it. The key words are: who, where, when, why, what, how.

Type of Question: Wide-open
Examples: What do others think?
What does anyone think about that?
What does anyone else think?
Answer: Any

Value: Very much—it stimulates maximum thought and relevant discussion. It is best used after an open question has just been answered.[1]

The last important evaluation of your question is how well it personally involves the hearer. The leader will increase the attendees' personal connection with the questioning as the discussion on the text transitions from abstract or unclear to the definite with application obvious. Jesus utilizes this technique to help His disciples to think objectively (not personally involved) then subjectively (with them personally involved) in the following passage.

Now Jesus and His disciples went out to the towns of Caesarea Philippi; and on the road He asked His disciples, saying to them, "Who do men say that I am?" And they answered, "John the Baptist; but some say, Elijah; and others, one of the prophets." He said to them, "But who do you say that I am?" And Peter answered and said to Him, "You are the Christ" (Mk. 8:27-29, NKJV).

The Lord got His disciples thinking about who "others" said He was to enable them to think more clearly in expressing who they felt He was. By cooperatively developing the group's textual understanding and personal involvement, the leader creates an application crescendo that will be sure to stick in the minds of the group for some time to come.

13

Helpful Hints for Leaders

Through experience in leading group Bible studies, a natural list of lessons learned will develop. If you take note of what was learned through these lessons, the likelihood of repeat mistakes is diminished. Here are some practical tips from my experiences (successes and failures) in leading small group Bible studies.

Weekly studies generally work the best. Bible studies every other week do not lend themselves to building good study routines. Many will still wait until the night before the group meeting to do the lesson. By then, much from two weeks earlier is forgotten. It takes more review in this type of study to keep it afloat. It is also easier for people to "cool off" and not return in a bi-weekly study than in a weekly study where commitment and discovery remains more active.

Have people sit in an informal circle or around a table. The circle should be as tight has possible to inspire intimacy. Be sure everyone can see each other. Participants should not have to raise their voices, which can be interpreted as aggressive, just to be heard in the study.

The room should be well lit. Good lighting enhances the atmosphere and allows people to read more easily. Realtors use this technique in showing homes for sale.

Ensure that the room is properly ventilated and has good heating/cooling control. Finding the comfort range for a study group can be difficult, but perhaps just a little cooler is better than being too hot. In one of our home Bible studies, we had a married couple of temperature extremes. Normally, she would wear a sweater (sometimes even in the summer), and he would have a little cloth to dry the sweat off his forehead during a study session. The solution: a small fan was placed on a table and aimed directly at him, while she sipped hot tea during the study. It would be interesting to know how they survive together at home.

The meeting should start on time and end on time. We have found that starting studies at 6:45 is better than 7:00. For some reason, people are more on time for the 6:45 study.

Pray for God's blessing on the study and your ability to lead the study with love, while remaining true to God's Word. Pray for opportunities within your sphere of associations to make contacts with the lost and perhaps start a study together. Most of my outreach studies have started with one to five people. The studies normally grow from there.

It may be encouraging to have different participants open and close a discipleship study in prayer, but make sure that the believer is comfortable doing so or he may be highly embarrassed. In an outreach study usually I will open and close the study in prayer. Never ask an unsaved person to pray aloud (Jn. 9:31). The teacher would be giving a confused message. Without believing the gospel, they do not have the Holy Spirit as a spiritual link or Christ as High Priest in order to gain an audience with the Father.

Seek group commitment in the first study. The first study should include an open discussion about what will be studied, what different individuals are looking for from the study, how much time it will take during the week to do the study justice, and how many weeks the study will meet (suggest eight to twelve weeks). I strongly recommend a definite length in a study period. The unsaved will usually not commit if they think they are getting into a long commitment.

Have an ordered plan of study. Short tangents are okay, but be careful not to drift too far from the topic. If you don't finish the planned study material, you lose the accountability of the attendee being in the Word to answer questions for next week's study. It is hard for some to get back into a regular study pattern if they have had a week off. Always have the questions for the next week's study available at the current group meeting.

Memorize scriptures together as a group. A technique that works well for stimulating memorization is to have one or two verses each week to memorize which are pertinent to the lesson. Coordinated group memorization can be achieved by typing out a full list of the verses to be memorized by the group over a period of time. The verses need to be correlated with the planned study agenda (e.g., by chapters or books or lesson numbers). It is best if the memory verses relate to the particular study material that week.

Going over memory verses together is a great way to pass a few minutes if someone is late. We take turns asking each other past memory verses. This gives accountability. This activity often generates a few laughs and sets a nice tone to start the study.

Read the passage of Scripture to be studied aloud. I have found that having each person read one verse at a time around the circle keeps everyone involved and listening. You need not read a whole chapter if the passage is difficult or has natural breaks or subject changes (read only a digestible amount of Scripture at one time). Remember, *"Faith cometh by hearing and hearing by the Word of God"* (Rom. 10:17). God's Word, not discussion of God's Word, should be central to the study. The leader should probably discuss the background and theme of the passage, then begin discussing it as a group through active questioning. Reading the Word aloud first will reacquaint folks with the passage and help alleviate spurious answers to questions.

Be a good listener. God gave us two ears and one mouth; perhaps He wanted us to listen twice as much as talk. Listening shows love. Be available to meet privately with an attendee who is lingering behind after the study is over. Perhaps ask them, "You seem to be a bit preoccupied tonight. Is their anything you would like to talk about?" I have seen people burst into tears after I have asked this question, or one like it. They were waiting for someone to notice and take an interest in them. These one-on-one moments are when people seem to make the most progress in coming to the Saviour! If an after-study environment is not conducive for a quiet visit, invite the attendee to dinner sometime during the next week and visit afterwards, or visit them in their own home.

We have seen several people come to know the Saviour through after-dinner conversations in our home. One particular event sticks in my mind. We were taking a Christian man (saved two-and-a-half years earlier in an after-dinner discussion) with us to a Bible conference in Detroit. My wife and I wanted to have a short visit with a married couple we had seen come to Christ nine years earlier (the husband also was saved in an after-dinner experience). It was quite a moment when at the door of their Detroit home these two men met. One man looked at the other and said, "I know you." The other man said, "You're right; I know you, too. We used to go bar-hopping together, but now I'm saved." As these two men rejoiced together in sharing their salvation experience, one man smiled and said, "So you fell for the 'come over for dinner' thing, too!" The Lord often sought to reach one soul at a time (see John 3—Nicodemus and John 4—a Samaritan woman). Is there one hungry soul you can invite over for dinner?

The study is about others learning, not about exposing your knowledge. The study leader should help those attending discover the answer, instead of answering all the questions. The answer will be much more real to them if they have dug it out rather than just being told what it is.

Don't shortchange quiet moments. There is a tendency for people to become uncomfortable during quiet moments and perhaps even more of a tendency for the leader to answer his/her own question. Allow people time to think; God may be dealing with them in the stillness of the moment.

Be honest in every aspect of the study. If you don't know an answer, don't contrive one. Giving an answer "off the cuff" can damage your credibility as a teacher if you're wrong. Simply say, "That's a great question and I wish I had a great answer, but I don't. Please let me study the matter and I will get back with you next week." Then *get back with them* next week. If you don't address the question at the next study, some might question your integrity or think that you're dodging a particular portion of the Bible because it conflicts with your faith. By getting back to the group with an answer, you demonstrate that you are a learner also. If it is a question that the group can study out, then why not put the question to the group for the following week's discussion.

James affirms what great accountability with God a teacher of His word has (Jas. 3:1). A teacher is speaking for God when he speaks from God's Word. This must be kept in mind when leading a Bible study. If you are addressing an area that is not dealt with specifically by Scripture, preface your answer with: "This is my opinion on the subject…" Perhaps you may even acknowledge other sound viewpoints on that subject to create an atmosphere of fairness and openness.

Be careful not to over-evaluate answers. It is very important in an outreach study to ensure that everyone feels they are contributing to the study. If someone doesn't answer the question put to them properly, don't say, "That does not answer my question." Instead remark, "You have touched on a very important point (or topic). So we don't lose track of where we are, why don't we table that thought for just a moment until we finish the subject at hand." Then, repeat the original question a bit differently, and pose it to the group. After the question has properly been handled, return to the "off track" subject that was introduced.

Cross references to other passages should be encouraged if a study group consists of all Christians. However, in an evangelistic outreach study, try to limit thumbing all through the Bible to answer questions. Over the years of Bible study teaching, we have met several people who did not know there was an Old Testament and a New Testament in the Bible. Looking up each passage was like an expedition into unknown scriptural jungles. It will likely be necessary to look up a few other passages during a study, but don't overdo it. Some will be embarrassed about not finding Scripture passages, while others may think that understanding the biblical principle is a very complex process. The gospel is not complex, and we should not make it complex to the hearer.

Watch for facial expressions. This form of communication is very important for the leader to observe and respond to. If the teacher misses the non-verbal, he or she may be forced to handle the more difficult verbal communication. A person's facial expressions will tell you if they don't understand, disagree, are bored, excited, tired, or even afraid. Use good judgment. If someone is tired or has had a hard day, go easy on him with questioning during the study. If someone is bored, try to use an illustration or a personal story to perk up interest. Some will be afraid of the Bible study for a while (perhaps a saved spouse has encouraged an unsaved spouse to come). For this person, a tender touch on the shoulder, a warm smile, a cup of tea, a personal interest in them and a little humor will go a long way toward putting them at ease.

Try to sense if someone has something to share but doesn't quite have the courage to say it. If someone is rereading a passage of Scripture or frantically thumbing through the Bible looking for some long lost passage while at the same time shaking their head, stop and get them on board. They may not be understanding, or may even be disagreeing with you. Go on together as a group; don't leave people straggling behind.

Watch for changing body posture. This is also important non-verbal communication. If an attendee abruptly sits up in their chair or leans quickly forward or crosses their arms or closes their Bible, you might have a pride issue to deal with. It is normal for human pride to be in opposition to the things of God, so expect that it will occasionally elevate its ugly head.

As the Holy Spirit convicts an unsaved soul of the truth, it is natural for the flesh to rebel. The attendees' belief system is being whittled away by God and at some point will be so fragile that it will begin to totter. This creates fear in the unsaved attendee. Sometimes this fear manifests itself as anger at the study leader as the unsaved soul again tries to strengthen the flimsy religious framework they are desperately holding onto. It is best to work with this person one-on-one after the study or perhaps visit them in their home after their emotions have simmered down. However, if this is not possible, resort to the tactic that the Lord used with the lawyer in Luke 10. Simply ask questions and have them read Scripture. If you get a wrong answer, ask them to read the Scripture again. In this way, you limit the argument to between them and God. They cannot argue with you because you are just facilitating the Word and asking questions. You are not making any statements or conclusions.

It may be helpful to have another believer host an evangelical study if that will make your neighbors more comfortable. However, never ask an unbeliever to host the study. If they back out, you might be stuck with no place to meet or at the home of a another non-believer, who could back out a week or two later. It is best to host the study in your own home or in the home of another couple committed to the Lord and this type of ministry.

If space allows and help is available, include a children's program along with the adult outreach study. Although older children are encouraged to attend a discipleship study of adult believers, we have found that children in an adult outreach study tend to hinder a sense of oneness. The adults feel constrained from talking about real adult issues when children are present. Secondly, the study can expose children unnecessarily to bad language and worldly mischief.

For the last twelve years, my wife and I have doubleteamed to teach a weekly adult and children's study. This gives us two opportunities at retaining the unsaved in the study. Even if the parents are not too excited about coming to the study, they will likely continue coming if their children enjoy themselves. An hour-long children's program of singing, Bible memorization, a Bible lesson, perhaps a missionary story, and an art or craft project pertaining to the lesson, makes a great agenda. Then allow a few minutes for treats and a game while the adults are finishing up.

Don't just babysit children during the adult study; God has given you their souls for gospel outreach as well. Statistically, they are more likely to receive the Lord as their personal Saviour than the parents are. Be sure to keep the two studies far enough apart so as not to distract from the adult study.

If a man and woman (whom you don't know) come together to an evangelistic outreach study, don't assume and don't ask if they are married. Look for two wedding rings and listen well when they introduce themselves. It can create a tense moment for the whole group if it comes out that they are living in sin together. The US Census Bureau reported in 1988 that there were 2.3 million unmarried co-habitating couples, so don't be surprised if unmarried couples who live together come to a study. If one comes to Christ and the other one doesn't, it can create a serious situation for the group study and certainly for the couple. With the understanding of God's will, the saved individual should desire to terminate the sinful living pattern and follow the Lord. This will likely require special one-on-one time with the couple to work through the situation, as there may be financial, property, and living accommodation difficulties.

Pick your battles carefully. The majority of religious errors or traditions that are expressed in a group study are not worth commenting on. You can simply respond, "Yes, that is what the _____ Catechism teaches." If the subject is salvation related, you should address it through various scriptures. However, if it isn't (praying to saints vs. Christ alone), let it pass and deal with it later.

Sometimes people express religious sayings or make

gestures before and after prayer. Let it go. The goal is to keep them coming, so they will be exposed to the Word through the week as they prepare for the study. Once we had a couple over for dinner. Immediately after one of our children gave thanks for the food, the father led his family in a religious prayer. My response was, "We can never be too thankful for what God has provided for us."

If someone in the study pulls you aside and shares something with you in confidence, keep it that way. By repeating anything (even to your spouse), you run the risk of gossip starting and of undermining the trusting relationship you are trying to build with that person. If you are unsure whether it should be shared as a prayer request with other Christians, ask the individual if he/she would like others to be praying about it specifically. Then, be sure to understand how much of their situation should be divulged if they desire others to pray. Remember, you don't have to release all the details for people to be knowledgeable in praying for someone. God already knows more about it than you do, or what others need to know.

Never pressure someone into a decision to receive Christ. The Lord said, *"The wind bloweth where it listeth, and thou hearest the sound thereof, but canst not tell whence it cometh, and whither it goeth: so is every one that is born of the Spirit"* (Jn. 3:8). The study leader can pray and pose questions, giving opportunity to the unsaved soul to repent and accept Christ's substitutionary death for their sins, but cannot save them. If the study leader, through high-pressure tactics, gets a false profession from an attendee, they will be worse off than before. Besides remaining unregenerated, the rehearsed confession you wrangled out of them may hinder any true, heartfelt repentance in the future. In short, you have contributed to a spiritual abortion!

When leading someone to Christ, don't have the person repeat a memorized prayer. A drowning man has no problem expressing his cries for help. If God convinces the unsaved attendee that he truly is lost and headed for hell, he will cry out to God to be saved based on the knowledge that he needs a Saviour. Prayer is the soul expressing to God what he knows and what he needs. When leading a man to Christ, don't put words into his mouth. Have him pray aloud from his heart. People are not saved by praying a prayer. Trusting in Christ saves them. It is a heart matter.

There have been occasions when the person in the middle of their prayer will say, "What else do I need to say?" or "Did I say enough?" This usually stems from years of religious rote and works-based salvation teaching. Simply respond, "God heard the words you spoke, but more importantly He saw the depths of your heart. If you believe you're a sinner and received Jesus Christ as your only way to heaven, then God promises to save you, and you have passed from death to life (Jn. 5:24)." I usually pray aloud after they pray to reinforce their knowledge of the gospel message and clarify anything not quite right in their prayer. Don't try to perfect their prayer life. The new believer is going to say things that are not quite right, but what joy there is in the simplicity of a repentant heart!

If you are privileged to witness someone turn to Christ, don't steal the new convert's opportunities to tell others about it. This robs him of occasions to strengthen his faith. Paul acknowledged the necessity of believing with the heart unto righteousness and confession of the mouth unto salvation (Rom. 10:10). Although water baptism doesn't save us or wash our sins away, Peter acknowledges that there is a salvation in it (1 Pet. 3:21). Water baptism has a saving effect to the mind. When Satan comes, casting doubts on the security of your soul, you look back and remember a time when you stood in front of a group of people and proclaimed what God had done for you and, in obedience to Christ's command, you were baptized. Likewise, every time a new convert shares his testimony it strengthens his faith.

Don't let an outreach study be dominated by Christians. One or two Christians to help support discussion is good, but unsaved attendees will feel too much pressure if surrounded by evangelicals. Also, Christians are often quick to give the answers, which cuts short the discovery experience for non-believers. Too many Christians in an outreach study will stifle the outreach goal intended.

Ensure that the group does not become a clique, especially if your Bible study is just among believers in your local assembly. This is why it is good to put limits on the study group and to try to have new people come in from time to time. If a clique develops, it will be wise to disband the study for the good of the local assembly. The local church needs all believers using their gifts to minister to each other, not subsets of isolated Christians serving only one another.

Maintain a global doctrinal focus. Don't let the group drift into select modes of thinking or patterns. The group may become so "caring" that time together becomes a shar-

ing time of personal testimonies instead of a study of biblical truth. A good Bible study will not overlook the main
theme of the Bible: God brings redemption and restoration
to the human race through the sacrifice of His Son Jesus
Christ. Too much focus on self or sharing of problems will
lead to a diminished understanding of deeper doctrines of
Scripture.

14

Securing Relationships

One of the notable fallacies of the small group Bible study movement over the last thirty years is the over-emphasis on the need to "affirm" group members to retain them. In some studies, the focus of making everyone feel a part and accepted is so strong that exhortations concerning sin and proper Christian conduct become second place.

One prominent Christian magazine in addressing how to lead Bible study groups even made affirming others an affirmation for study success: "Thou shalt: Learn to affirm one another...We need to say sincerely to others, 'I think you are really special.'"[1]

It is important to be sensitive to attendees' needs and to be compassionate concerning their pains, but not to the exclusion of God or the personal holiness He demands of His children. If we are not careful, it is possible that seeking Christian friendships becomes primary over seeking God. Theologian J. I. Packer believes that when churches encourage people to join small groups now, as opposed to twenty-five years ago, "It is not so much thought of as a way of seeking God as much as seeking Christian friends. The vertical axis is not emphasized as much as the horizontal axis."[2] Some groups become so focused on "affirming" people to create a sense of community that they forget to consult God's Word to affirm how He feels about the person and their problems.

It is true that God is love (1 Jn. 4:8). But God is also holy. His holiness is never discarded because of His love. If God would not spare the obedient Lord Jesus from judgment when our sin was placed on Him, He certainly will not overlook a disobedient child of God in rebellion against Him. Paul makes it clear that Christians are not to have close contact with someone professing to be a Christian that willingly behaves in a way that disgraces God (2 Thess. 3:6). If a man professes to be a Christian and has been exhorted and reproved, he should be removed from close fellowship with believers (personal contact, the local church, and a Bible study group) until he has repented (1 Cor. 5:4-13). If a rebellious Christian is allowed to remain in your study group, your pursuit of the God of peace is over.

It is a different matter with an unbeliever. You would expect the ungodly to behave in an ungodly way. We can accept and love people for who they are despite what they do, but we should never condone what they do to make them accepted and loved.

Whether an evangelical Bible study or a discipleship study with young Christians, it is important to secure relationships. Your friendship may be the only reason that unsaved person returns next week to the Bible study. The relationship you build with a new convert will provide the necessary level of trust it takes to usher him or her into local church fellowship. As already explored in this book, the Lord Jesus was not afraid to associate and make connections with the unsaved. Yet, these associations should never result in a compromise of our faith or convictions.

Concerning Christian fellowship, here are a few biblical principles which should make nurturing relationships in small groups both a beneficial and happy experience:

1. Bearing one another's burdens (Gal. 6:2).
2. Encouraging each other (Heb. 10:24).
3. Being concerned for each others interests (Phil. 2:4).
4. Admonishing one another (1 Thess. 5:14).
5. Exhorting one another daily (Heb. 3:13).
6. Being affectionate to one another (Rom. 12:10).
7. Praying for one another (Col. 4:2, 12).
8. Loving and giving to one another (Rom. 13:8).

To accomplish this degree of fellowship, Christians must be regularly gathering together. As they gather, relationships are secure because hearts are beating as one in Christ. Brethren intimately know one another, their needs and burdens. This type of fellowship guarantees believers won't be able to slip into the easy chair of a comfortable life or into isolation to practice sin (Prov. 18:1).

The Creator has programmed basic needs deep within our human fabric. We need to feel secure and important. We need to have intimacy with others. But our deepest need is to have a relationship with God Himself. For the unbelieving attendee, the leader can help nurture the former needs, but only God can fill the emptiness of the human spirit.

One way to demonstrate to attendees that you care for them and that they are important to you is to regularly keep contact with them between studies (phone or e-mail). Use your home to have them over for dinner. Show them the love of Christ, and they will keep coming back.

15

Handling Problem Situations

THE TRAIN IS OFF THE TRACKS

If the study is wandering farther and farther away from the intended subject, you will need to simply call everyone's attention to it through a verbal recognition of the situation or by a thought-provoking question. Short tangents are fine, but they should not overshadow the planned study material or the study will not finish on time or the planned material will not get covered. Either of these can cause further study problems. If parents have school-aged children in the children's study, they may not come back if the studies continually drag on past the children's bedtimes. Also, if the study material does not get covered, the accountability of written questions (being in the Word through the week) is lost. Studies need order to survive.

THE UGLY ANSWER

Never contradict a person flatly, or you may discourage them from coming to the study again. There are tactful ways of securing right answers. Try one of the following four techniques:

If there are other mature Christians in the group, you

113

might try to redirect the same question back to the group. For example, the leader might respond, "This is not an easy question; let's ponder that thought for a moment longer while we explore other Scripture. Did anyone else find some helpful verses addressing the question?" As each person responds to this question, be careful to summarize and steer the group to the correct scriptural conclusion. Remember, however, that the teacher is learning too, and that there may be some aspect of the question that you have not thought of. The unplanned answer to your question might be a legitimate, good answer. This is a great time for the class to see a little humility and that you are learning just like them. Perhaps you could respond with, "That is a great answer; I wish I had thought of it!"

A second method is to try to find some element of truth in the answer given and build on it to get to the right answer. This gives the person who responded some satisfaction that they are contributing to the group discussion; and it keeps them coming back.

For example, someone answers "Joseph" to the question, "Who was the real father of Jesus?" The teacher might respond, "Yes, it is true that Joseph was Jesus' earthly father, but we know from these scriptures that Jesus was begotten of God and born to the virgin Mary. So God, not Joseph, was Jesus' true Father."

A third method is to again acknowledge some element of truth in what they have said or perhaps even paraphrase a bit what they have said to create an element of truth to build on. Then, have the person who gave the answer reread the passage aloud or read another passage of Scripture, and ask them questions about what they have just read to guide the formulation of the correct answer. The art of posing the right question is very important in stimulating spiritual understanding. The Lord Jesus used this technique in addressing the lawyer in Luke 10:26.

A fourth method is required for a really bad answer. If the answer is so far off that there is no hope of finding a thread of truth to build on, apologize for the way the question was worded and try to pose the question from a different angle. Keep them talking and then when you eventually hear something true to build on, turn to the Bible and construct a sound answer. Remember wholesome humor and sacrificing of self will get you out of almost any tough situation, no matter how bad the answer is.

THE DIFFICULT PERSON

I grew up working on a cattle ranch in Kansas. I was given instruction on how to work closely with cattle and survive. My boss told me you either keep right up next to them or clear away. It is in that mid-area that you will get the stuffing kicked out of you. It took getting knocked flat twice to learn the lesson, and I never got kicked again. I have learned that handling a difficult person is a lot like handling a disagreeable cow; you either stay right next to them or clear away. So the seating of the study is very important. You want to sit right next to the difficult person. Human tendency is to generally not raise your voice in conversation or be as rude to someone sitting right next to you. The worst possible location is directly across the table from you. The table between you helps facilitate a perceived barrier between you and them.

Another technique for defusing a difficult person who wants to get a rise out of you is to apply Proverb 15:1: *"A soft answer turneth away wrath, but grievous words stir up anger."* Even if this individual insults your grandmother, you respond only in a soft, low-volume voice and with cor-

115

dial words. Don't let Satan get the victory in your conversation by enticing you to lose your cool. Keep in mind the big picture and pray. I use this technique in marriage counseling. If a couple starts to raise their voices, I simply say, "Let's whisper for a while" (which is a stated ground rule). Usually, the couple will be forced to smile at the situation, and the tension is broken.

Several years ago, while I was in aerospace engineering, I had to give a series of technical presentations to a major aircraft company with which we had secured a contract. Our company was non-compliant on several contractual issues, and the general consensus among my co-workers was that I was going to be burnt at the stake or tarred and feathered. However, in the process of traveling across the country to give this report, there was sufficient time for me to completely lose my voice. For two days, I had a room full of people sitting as close to me as possible while I whispered to them the details. There was not one tense moment in all the meetings! As a matter of fact, many started whispering too, and we got along fine.

The Lord has graciously allowed the author to lead hundreds of small group studies. In that time, I have never had to ask anyone to leave, and there have only been two individuals who created an intense situation during a study. Tender, soft responses and resorting to reading Scripture aloud and asking questions will usually control a difficult situation. Don't lose the leadership position of the study. Work with the person as much as possible one-on-one outside the study (2 Tim. 2:14).

Those who continue to be cantankerous are either trying to impress others with their knowledge or are naturally argumentative. In either case, if you stick to the "read and question" strategy, their foolishness becomes so pronounced to the group, and eventually to themselves, that they will either quit arguing or quit coming.

THE TALKER

The following advice is given by Paul Fromer:

Some people are compulsive talkers. They always have to be saying something. The result is that they make a shambles of the discussion. Good discussion is group exploration of a passage and the talker shrinks this down to a monologue. Why does a talker talk? Generally because he's never learned to discuss. He doesn't know how to work with others to figure out a passage.

You may need to take him aside and explain the nature of the study. Ground rule #3 helps here (give everyone a chance to talk). Show the talker why it is necessary.

The talker may have been a teacher, trained in the idea that teaching equals telling. Show him that this study is to help the member discover things in the passage for himself. Suggest that he hold back to give someone else the chance to discover the passage's meaning. Bear in mind that taking the talker aside to speak to him privately is a last resort and it is wise to try other things in the group first.

I've sometimes asked at the beginning of a study when I knew a talker was present, "If you know the answer to a question, how do you decide whether to answer it?" This is usually a shock to the talker because he thinks that the single condition for answering a question is that he knows the answer. The group can quickly correct that misunderstanding and generally solve the problem in advance.

If the talker still talks too much (and if you've done all the things above), it will be necessary to caution him publicly by saying gently and with a smile, "No, Joe, give everyone a chance to talk. We have fifty minutes and ten people, so on the average you have about five minutes. Be sure to use it wisely."[1]

Personally, I have encountered many more "talkers" than

"contentious" folks in leading studies. These are generally nice folks who just like to be heard by others. However, a mature Christian will learn that listening is to sacrifice your right to express so someone else can. It is a form of giving and shows love. A wise person will refrain his lips and speak when he/she has something to say and carefully listen while others are speaking. I have found that using "direct" or "relay" questions help direct airtime away from the "talker" to others. Another tactic is to quickly cut in when they finally take a breath of air!

> *In the multitude of words there lacketh not sin, but he that refraineth his lips is wise* (Prov. 10:19). *He that answereth a matter before he heareth it, it is folly and shame unto him* (Prov. 18:13).

Someone Proposes Studying a Not-so-Sound Book

This may happen if you rely on prepackaged teaching materials. Although I generally start with a study book (like the BCT) for discipling new converts or in an evangelical outreach study, I normally get directly into the Bible after that for two reasons. First of all, it is the Word of God, and I know I will not have any problem with what the author writes. Secondly, if I continue to use study books instead of a Scripture study, sooner or later I am inviting someone in the group to suggest a study book I have never heard of. Do you take a chance? Absolutely not! Don't go there!

Unless you are completely familiar with the book and the publisher (knowing publishers will tell you a lot about the doctrines and the general flavor likely in the study materials), don't use it. You risk derailing the study if some unsound doctrine is introduced. The unsaved don't have the Spirit of God to teach them, and no doubt Satan, who planted the lie, will lead some away after it.

16

Blessings of a Small Group Bible Study

It is my hope that this book has stimulated you to share the good news of Jesus Christ with the unsaved and to continue discipling those who respond. This is the command of the Lord, and the great desire of His heart. The small group Bible study is one successful means of practically accomplishing the Great Commission.

What are some of the blessings of small group studies?

They provide a means of reaching the unchurched. The primary purpose of a home Bible study is to provide a community-centered place for evangelism. Many people will not venture into a church meeting, but will attend a study in a friend's home. The informal and hospitable atmosphere of the home can draw people in to hear the gospel and make an intelligent decision concerning the Saviour.

They can be a spiritual nursery for discipleship. The home environment allows for great flexibility in teaching and training new converts. It is my custom to give a note-book to new converts shortly after they come to Christ. I ask them to carry this notebook with them wherever they go and to write down every question that comes to mind. When they feel they have enough questions for a visit, they call me, and we try to get together as soon as we can. One new believer named Lee called me and wanted an hour of my time to go through his first questions in his blue note-book. I invited him to come our home. We sat down at the kitchen table to discuss his questions and remained there for nearly four hours. Time flies when you're searching and discovering spiritual mysteries for the first time!

They offer a method of assimilating people into church life. This is especially important for those people who have been saved out of a religious setting of rote and tradition. It is hard for these folks to engage in worship from the heart and be active in a local assembly when they have only known dead "pomp and circumstance" all their lives. It is hard to assimilate new Christians into a New Testament patterned church meeting without spending some time teaching them the biblical design for churches. Because this transition may be radical in nature for the new believer, I don't normally encourage new believers to attend church meetings until they are digesting the Word of God properly and understand New Testament principles for gathering. When they see these truths for themselves and are ready to put them into practice, then they are ready to move from the spiritual nursery into active church fellow-ship. For some this natal discipleship may only require a few days; for others it will be several weeks.

They are a training ground to test and exercise spiri-tual gift. Within a year of starting a workplace Bible study with three individuals, our group had grown to about twelve or fifteen people. Within this group, there were several new converts and many young Christians. Although this study had started as an evangelistic outreach, it was obvious that the goal had changed. The lost had either gotten saved or weeded themselves out over time. This study had now become strictly a discipleship study.

From time to time, smaller evangelistic studies were held on different days over the lunch hour, and new Christians were added to the bigger discipleship study at the conclusion of the evangelical study. This study was the perfect place to challenge Christians in the realm of teaching. For some, it was obvious that they didn't have a teaching gift, and for others, their teaching gift was apparent, exercised and developed. This study is still meeting weekly and has produced a half-dozen able teachers and two men that are now in church leadership. Two or three times a year, I visit the group just to keep in contact with the men.

A discipler should have the goal of working himself out of a job. The new convert must be a disciple of Christ, who is able to introduce others to Christ and disciple them. The small group study is a great place to test and develop a teaching gift.

Bible studies are good places to engage prodigal children in coming back to God! Prodigals often don't do well under the pressure of large group environments after being alone for so long. Perhaps pull up an empty chair in your Bible study and pray for God to fill the chair with someone who needs to be in the study. The empty chair will serve as an active reminder to pray.

These are all great reasons for engaging in the ministry of small group Bible studies. However, the best reason is that it complies with the Lord's command to evangelize. Every believer has been commanded by the Lord to preach the gospel and disciple those responding (Mt. 28:18-20).

The Lord asked the following question of His disciples, *"Why do you call Me, Lord, Lord, and do not the things that I say?"* (Lk. 6:46). Don't call Him Lord if you are not obeying His commands and following His example. Are you obeying the Great Commission?

Perhaps God is tugging on your heart to initiate an evangelical study in your home or work place. Perhaps you have been encouraged to make some changes in your present small group study to ensure it continues to prosper and grow. Whatever God is calling you to do, be obedient to Him.

Appendix

The Development of the Bible

THE OLD TESTAMENT

Concerning the history and canonization of the Old Testament, Norman L. Geisler and William E. Nix explain in their book, *A General Introduction to the Bible:*

> The standard critical theory has been that the books of the Hebrew Scriptures were canonized in three stages, according to their dates of composition, the Law (400 BC), Prophets (200 BC), and Writings (AD 100). However, this view is untenable in light of the fact that the complete canon, even with a threefold description, is known to have existed much earlier than AD 100, and possibly as early as 200 BC. In fact, Jesus in Luke 24:44 and Josephus both alluded to a threefold division of the Hebrew canon before AD 100. Furthermore, there is evidence that inspired books were added immediately to the canon as they were written.[1]

The first section of the Hebrew text was written by Moses, the second by the prophets; and the third, the

"Writings," by wise men, kings and priests. We owe a lot to Jewish scribes. Their tenacity and accuracy through the centuries preserved the inspired text. Copies of worn-out scrolls were hand-written, then each Hebrew letter was counted to ensure accuracy. How do we know that the Old Testament text has been preserved in accuracy? Geisler and Nix comment:

> The various ancient translations of the Old Testament provide the textual scholar with valuable witness to the text. The Septuagint (Greek translation of the Old Testament), for example, preserves a textual tradition from the third century BC, and the Samaritan Pentateuchal tradition may date from the fifth century BC. These and the Masoretic text (fourth century AD) provide three Old Testament textual traditions, which, when critically evaluated, supply an overwhelming support for the integrity of the Old Testament text.[2]

THE NEW TESTAMENT

Testimony to the fidelity of the New Testament comes primarily from three sources: Greek manuscripts, ancient translations, and patristic citations (quotations from the Bible books by the early Church "Fathers").

The Greek manuscripts is the most important and can be subdivided into three classes, commonly termed the papyri, the uncials, and the minuscules. The most distinguishing feature of each has been chosen for these designations, for the papyrus (early paper made from compressed strips of rushes) manuscripts were also written in uncial letters. The second and third classes are differentiated by the style of writing, since both used vellum (usually calfskin) or parchment (sheep or goat skins) as the writing substance.[3]

Consider the following manuscripts in existence today which overwhelmingly validate the authenticity of the New Testament. The term "manuscript" is normally used for a handwritten literary composition, in contrast to a printed copy.

Of the seventy-six papyri manuscripts of the New Testament known today, the following three are given as important representatives:

John Rylands Fragment (Manchester, England; dated 117-138 AD) This papyrus piece was found in Egypt and is written on both sides. It contains five verses from the Gospel of John (18:31-33, 37-38).

Chester Beatty Papyri (Beatty Museum near Dublin, Ireland; dated 250 AD) It consists of three codices (singular, codex, a manuscript bound as a book rather than in scroll form) which contains most of the New Testament. The first portion is comprised of thirty leaves (the original had approximately 220) of a papyrus codex and contains the four Gospel accounts and Acts. The second section contains eighty-six slightly damaged leaves (104 in the original). This section contains the book of Hebrews and the Pauline epistles (excluding portions of Romans, 1 and 2 Thessalonians and the short book of Philemon). The third section contains ten slightly damaged leaves (the original had 32), which give us Revelation 9:10-17:2.

Bodmer Papyri (Library of World Literature at Culagny; dated 175 to 225 AD) This manuscript also consists of three codices dating back to 200 AD or earlier. The first portion includes 104 leaves of John's Gospel. The second section contains the earliest known copies of Jude, 1 Peter and 2 Peter (third century AD). The third portion contains 102 of 144 original leaves and provides the earliest known copy of the book of Luke. The Gospel of John is also recorded in this codex.

Of the 297 uncial manuscripts of the New Testament known today, the following three are given as important representatives:

Codex Vaticanus (Vatican Library at Rome; dated mid fourth century) Perhaps the oldest uncial on parchment or vellum. This codex contains most of the Old Testament (LXX, the usual designation for the Septuagint, meaning 70, for the approximate number of scholars who translated the OT Hebrew into Greek) and the New Testament except from Hebrews 9:14 through Revelation and Mark 16:9-20 and John 7:53-8:11). In total, it is composed of 617 leaves for the Old Testament and 142 for the New Testament.

Codex Sinaiticus (British Museum; dated fourth century). Written on good vellum, made from antelope skins, this codex contains over half the Old Testament (LXX), and all of the New Testament, with the exception of Mark 16:9-20 and John 7:53-8:11.

Codex Alexandrinus (National Library of the British Museum; dated fifth century). It contains the entire Old Testament, except for a few mutilated leaves, and most of the New Testament (only Mt. 1:1-25:6, Jn. 6:50-8:52 and 2 Cor. 4:13-12:6 are missing).

Other early manuscripts and the above form what is called the "critical text," which most of the modern Bible translations are based on (plus some inputs from the Dead Sea Scrolls). The critical text represents an objective attempt to reconstruct the authentic Apostolic writings (autographs). It is a scientific approach to the question of integrity, and it concludes that the present Greek text (after Nestle) is probably over 99% accurate in reproducing the exact words of the autographs.[4]

The King James Version of the Bible was based on the "received text" (or *Textus Receptus*), which was complied from available "majority" manuscripts at the time. The "received text" likely has its western roots is the Syrian Church.[5] The "majority" manuscripts are more numerous than the Alexandrian type which compose the critical text. The "majority" manuscripts date back to perhaps the 4th century to more generally the 9th century in origin. The New King James Version of the Bible was developed from the 1982 "majority text", which was complied from numerous "majority" manuscripts. If all types of textual variations are counted there are about 1800 differences between the "majority text" and "received text" and approximately 6500 between the "majority text" and "critical text" (which translates to 98% agreement). The bottom line—no substantial difference between these texts. Their differences are merely technical, not doctrinal, for the variants are doctrinally inconsequential because the whole of scripture declares the same truth. Thus, for all practical purposes, both texts convey the content of the autographs, even though they are separately garnished with their own minor scribal and technical differences.

Norman L. Geisler and William E. Nix conclude their analysis of New Testament authenticity:

It is sufficient to remember that while there are only 643 manuscripts by which the Iliad is reconstructed, nine or ten good ones for Caesar's Gallic Wars, twenty manuscripts of note for Livy's History of Rome, and only two by which Tacitus is known, yet there are about 5,000 Greek manuscripts to attest the New Testament....Most of the New Testament is preserved in manuscripts less than two hundred years from the original (portions of Chester Beatty Papyri), some books of the New Testament from little over one hundred years after their composition (portions of Bodmer Papyri), and one fragment comes within a generation of the first century (John Rylands Fragment).[6]

Besides these ancient Greek manuscripts of the New Testament, there are numerous hand-written portions of the Scripture existing today in other languages. Many of these date back to the infant days of the Church age.

The multitude of early copies of the Bible demonstrates not only the universality of Christianity, but the antiquity of the biblical text. These early versions provide some of the earliest copies of the complete canon of Scripture, and in many cases they outdate the manuscripts in Greek.

The Syrian church, for example, had begun its Peshitta in the second century. Titian's Diatessaron dates back to a time prior to AD 170. Soon after that time, in the third century and following, other versions began to appear in Egypt and the area near the Mediterranean Sea. Hence, the early existence of the Ethiopic, Coptic, Sahidic, Bohairic, Gothic, Arabic and other versions provides ample evidence of the presence of the entire Bible during the second, third and fourth centuries.[7]

Many of the modern versions also have input from the Dead Sea Scrolls found since 1947 in the Middle East, which have wonderfully validated the preservation of the Old Testament. R. Laird Harris, in his book, *Inspiration and Canonicity of the Bible,* writes:

> Since 1947 our direct knowledge of the Old Testament in pre-Christian times has been greatly increased as a result of the findings of the Dead Sea Scrolls. From 130 BC to 68 AD the Essene community on the northwest shore of the Dead Sea was evidently busily engaged in copying the Scriptures. Their town of Qumran has been excavated, and the bench and the table at which the scribes sat, even their very inkwells and pens, have been found. Several caches of

documents, stored by the scribes for safety in near-by caves, have been discovered. There is, therefore, no doubt regarding the general date of the documents, and the abundance of material has allowed those who specialize in paleography to arrange a sequence of hand-writing styles so as to date, with considerable certainty, manuscripts copied in these years.

Reports now indicate that all of our Old Testament books are represented among the Dead Sea Scrolls (perhaps with the exception of Esther, ed.). The best known is the first scroll of Isaiah, a beautiful and complete copy of the book, whose date may now safely be placed before 100 BC. It is of great value, and, as previously explained, its value is largely confirmatory of our Hebrew consonantal text. Fragments of Ecclesiastes have also been discovered which are said to date from about 150 BC....Also significant in the collection is a series of fragments of the Books of Samuel. These are said to date from around 200 BC, which would precede the Maccabean wars of independence. A further fragment of special interest is a portion of Leviticus which dates, according to Birnbaum, from about 400 BC.[8]

Endnotes

1. A Brief History of the Small Group Movement

1 Warren Bird, "The Great Small Group Takeover" *Christianity Today,* February 7, 1994, p. 27.

2 Ibid.

2. Christ's Touch

1 Howard G. Hendricks, "The Pastor and the Home Bible Classes" *The Pastors' Series 19* (Glen Ellyn: Scripture Press, 1967), p. 4.

3. Making Disciples through Evangelistic Studies

1 Susan Bergman, ed. *Martyrs* (San Francisco: Harper Collins).

5. The Study Leader

1 William Hendricks, "How Not to Kill Your Bible Study Discussions," *Moody Monthly,* April 1973, p. 47.

2 Albert Wollen, *How to Conduct Home Study Classes* (Scripture Press Publication Inc., 1969), p. 16.

6. Inviting Others and Getting Started

1 Ada Lum, *How to Begin an Evangelistic Bible Study* (Westmont, IL: InterVarsity Press, April 1972), p. 7.

7. The Hardest Study—The First One

1 Lyman Coleman, "The Hardest Study—Your First One" *Decision Magazine* (May 1991)

2 Howard G. Hendricks, *The Pastor and the Home Bible Classes* (Scripture Press Foundation, 1967).

8. Bibles, Study Aids and Materials

1 Edward J. Young, *Revelation and the Bible,* (Grand Rapids: Baker Book House, 1976), p. 167.

2 William MacDonald, *Believers Bible Commentary* (Nashville: Thomas Nelson Publishers, 1989), p. 17.

3 Dave Hunt, *A Woman Rides the Beast* (Eugene, OR: Harvest House Publishers, 1994), p. 477.

9. Teaching a Bible Study

1 Michael Wiebe, "The Anatomy of a Small Group," *His Magazine,* May 1976, p. 17.

2 "How to Lead a Small Group Bible Discussion," *The Navigators Log,* July 1971, p. 18.

3 Marilyn Kunz, "Bible Studies that Bring Them to Belief," *Christianity Today,* October 2, 1981, p. 21.

4 Lyman Coleman, "Effective Bible Study Groups—Real People Meeting Real Needs," *Decision Magazine,* May 1991, p. 9.

5 "How to Lead a Small Group Bible Discussion" et. al. p. 18.

10. Bibles Studies in the Workplace

1 Jack Houston, "Business People Take a Bible Break," *Moody Monthly,* July-August 1975, p. 78.

2 Stuart McAllister, "Put the Word to Work," *Moody Monthly,* March 1993, p. 67.

12. Questions, Questions, Questions

1 "How to Lead a Small Group Bible Discussion," *The Navigators Log,* July 1971, p. 18.

14. Securing Relationships

1 Lyman Coleman, "Effective Bible Study Groups—Real People Meeting Real Needs," *Decision Magazine,* May 1991, p. 9.

2 Warren Bird, "The Great Small Group Takeover," *Christian Today,* February 7, 1994, p. 29.

15. Handling Problem Situations

1 "Handling Problem Situations," *Moody Monthly,* June 1972, p. 99.

Appendix: the Development of the Bible

1. Norman L. Geisler and William E. Nix, *A General Introduction to the Bible* (Chicago: Moody Press, 1968) p. 151.

2 Ibid. p. 314.

3 Ibid. p. 268.

4 Ibid. p. 238.

5 Ibid. p. 390.

6 Ibid. p. 284.

7 Ibid. p. 287.

8 R. Laird Harris, *Inspiration and Canonicity of the Bible* (Grand Rapids: Zondervan, 1969), p. 135.